The Treasure of the Sierra Madre

Wisconsin/Warner Bros. Screenplay Series

The Treasure of the Sierra Madre

Edited with an introduction by

James Naremore

*Published for the Wisconsin Center for Film and Theater Research by
The University of Wisconsin Press*

Published 1979

The University of Wisconsin Press
114 North Murray Street
Madison, Wisconsin 53715

The University of Wisconsin Press, Ltd.
1 Gower Street
London WC1E 6HA, England

First printing

Printed in the United States of America

For LC CIP information see the colophon

ISBN 0-299-07680-6 cloth; 0-299-07684-9 paper

Contents

Foreword

In donating the Warner Film Library to the Wisconsin
Center for Film and Theater Research in 1969, along with the
RKO and Monogram film libraries and UA corporate records,
United Artists created a truly great resource for the study of
American film. Acquired by United Artists in 1957, during a
period when the major studios sold off their films for use on
television, the Warner library is by far the richest portion of
the gift, containing eight hundred sound features, fifteen
hundred short subjects, nineteen thousand still negatives,
legal files, and press books, in addition to screenplays for the
bulk of the Warner Brothers product from 1930 to 1950. For
the purposes of this project, the company has granted the
Center whatever publication rights it holds to the Warner
films. In so doing, UA has provided the Center another opportunity to advance the cause of film scholarship.

Our goal in publishing these Warner Brothers screenplays is
to explicate the art of screenwriting during the thirties and
forties, the so-called Golden Age of Hollywood. In preparing
a critical introduction and annotating the screenplay, the
editor of each volume is asked to cover such topics as the
development of the screenplay from its source to the final
shooting script, differences between the final shooting script
and the release print, production information, exploitation
and critical reception of the film, its historical importance, its
directorial style, and its position within the genre. He is also
encouraged to go beyond these guidelines to incorporate sup-
plemental information concerning the studio system of motion
picture production.

We could set such an ambitious goal because of the richness
of the script files in the Warner Film Library. For many film
titles, the files might contain the property (novel, play, short
story, or original story idea), research materials, variant drafts

7

of scripts (from story outline to treatment to shooting script), post-production items such as press books and dialogue continuities, and legal records (details of the acquisition of the property, copyright registration, and contracts with actors and directors). Editors of the Wisconsin/Warner Bros. Screenplay Series receive copies of all the materials, along with prints of the films (the most authoritative ones available for reference purposes), to use in preparing the introductions and annotating the final shooting scripts.

In the process of preparing the screenplays for publication, typographical errors were corrected, punctuation and capitalization were modernized, and the format was redesigned to facilitate readability. The illustrations are frame enlargements taken from a 35-mm print of the film provided by United Artists.

In theory, the Center should have received the extant scripts of all pre-1951 Warner Brothers productions when the United Artists Collection was established. Recent events, however, have created at least some doubt in this area. Late in 1977, Warners donated collections consisting of the company's production records and distribution records to the University of Southern California and Princeton University respectively. The precise contents of the collections are not known, since at the present time they are not generally open to scholars. To the best of our knowledge, all extant scripts have been considered in the preparation of these volumes. Should any other versions be discovered at a later date, we will recognize them in future printings of any volumes so affected.

Tino Balio
General Editor

Introduction: *A Likely Project*

James Naremore

It flashed through his mind that he had seen many a movie in which the hero was trapped in a situation like this. But he realized at the same time that he could not remember one single picture in which the producer had not done his utmost to help the trapped hero out again to save the girl from the clutches of a bunch of villains.

—B. Traven, *The Treasure of the Sierra Madre*

The worst ain't so bad when it finally happens. Not nearly as bad as you figure it will be before it's happened.

—Curtin in Huston's *The Treasure of the Sierra Madre*

The Treasure of the Sierra Madre, B. Traven's novel published in this country in 1935, tells the story of three down-and-out American working men stuck in Mexico at the end of an oil boom. Ragged and almost hopeless, they scrape together what money they have and set out to prospect for gold in the mountains. By extraordinary good fortune they strike it rich, but mutual suspicion, the harsh desert weather, and Mexican bandits all conspire to deprive them of their treasure. There is no Hollywood-style happy ending to the book, and, as the first quote above indicates, the very subject of movies is

9

sometimes used as a way of showing the disparity between life and fantasy. (At one point, two of the prospectors discuss using their gold to start up a movie theater in the town of their choice; the most untrustworthy of the two plans to be the entertainment director, leaving the more mundane details of management to his partner.) It is surprising, therefore, that Traven's novel should have become a classic motion picture from Warner Brothers and a winner of Academy Awards for best direction, best original screenplay, and best supporting actor and New York Film Critics prizes for best picture and best direction. Perhaps the prospector Curtin is correct: The worst ain't so bad when it finally happens.

On the other hand, it is easy to see why *Treasure* should have seemed a likely project for its screenwriter and director, John Huston, who was once known as a Hollywood maverick and who seems to have drifted into the movies from a life more lucky but no less vagrant than Traven's characters. Huston's films typically end in failure, though not necessarily in absolute disaster. The people in his stories are frequently involved in a dangerous quest—it may be a search for a jeweled falcon, a bank robbery, a journey down an African river aboard a battered steamboat, a mad chase after a white whale, or, most recently, an attempt to conquer an entire country and become its king. The best of these people behave with grace under pressure, but at the last moment some ironic twist usually makes everything go wrong, so they become philosophers of a sort, like losers at a roulette wheel. Thus Sam Spade, in a gesture Huston invented for him, wryly calls the phony black bird "the stuff that dreams are made of," and then walks sadly offscreen. Even when the characters do succeed, there is a moment toward the end of the story when all their striving comes to nothing and they have only their respect for one another as reward—for example, in *The African Queen*, where Bogart and Hepburn embrace and collapse on the deck of their boat in complete fatigue, the camera rising above high marsh grass to show the ocean they have sought only a few feet away. For Huston, the human adventure is always arbitrary, absurd, and cruel, but it can be partly redeemed by ironic distance, stubbornness, and let-the-chips-fall courage.

The quality of life in Huston's films clearly has roots in his own experience. He was born in 1906 in Nevada, Missouri, a town he claims his grandfather had won in a poker game. The son of actor Walter Huston and newspaperwoman Rhea Gore, he led an unstable and rather sickly childhood. His parents were divorced when he was quite young, and at one point he was confined to a sanitorium where he was diagnosed as hopelessly ill; at nights he began sneaking out of his room and taking devil-may-care slides for life down a nearby waterfall, which miraculously restored his health. Having survived this brush with death, he became an amiable vagabond, taking up risk as a style. As he grew older he gambled on horses, studied painting with an avant-garde group in Los Angeles, became an amateur boxing champion, acted on the stage in New York, and was made an honorary lieutenant in the Mexican cavalry. He then almost casually began a vocation as a writer by selling a few stories to H. L. Mencken at *The American Mercury*.

Shortly after his stories were published, Huston followed his father to the movie studios. After a brief period doing scripts at Universal, he made an abortive attempt at working for Gaumont-British in England, where he quarreled with his boss and was fired. On the same day, he discovered that a ticket he had bought for the Irish Sweepstakes was a winner, giving him just enough money to get his sick wife back to the States. He remained behind, living for a time a sort of Orwellian bum's existence in London, but by the late thirties he had moved again to Hollywood, where he quickly became an important writer at Warners (*Jezebel, Juarez, Sergeant York,* and *High Sierra,* among others). In 1941 he persuaded Jack Warner to let him direct his own adaptation of *The Maltese Falcon*, and that film, made at virtually the same time as *Citizen Kane,* gave him a debut almost as impressive as Orson Welles's. After directing two relatively minor pictures from other people's scripts (*In This Our Life* and *Across the Pacific*), he went to work for the U.S. Army film unit, where he enhanced his reputation with three of the most impressive, least patriotic of wartime documentaries—*Report from the Aleutians, The Battle of San Pietro,* and *Let There Be Light.*

Immediately after the war, he returned to Warners and began *The Treasure of the Sierra Madre,* which was his second feature as writer/director and the one that brought him the greatest number of personal awards. It still holds up as a spare, relatively uncompromised adaptation of the Traven novel, with a good feel for life in the Mexican provinces, a distinguished performance by Walter Huston, and a vivid, chilling portrayal of the bandit Gold Hat by Alfonso Bedoya. It is arguably Huston's most representative film, in various ways recalling *The Maltese Falcon* and looking forward to *The Man Who Would Be King.* It is also one of his most effective screenplays, as the script published here will show.

Treasure and *Falcon*: Their Common Themes

Huston had wanted to make a film of *The Treasure of the Sierra Madre* for some time, and Warners anticipated him by beginning an adaptation before he was demobilized from the war. (B. Traven, incidentally, was a relatively unknown writer inside the United States and was paid only five thousand dollars for the property. By contrast, when Walter Huston was signed on as an actor in the film, he was guaranteed a minimum of fifty thousand dollars for eight weeks' work.) According to some references, Robert Rossen wrote an early draft of the adaptation, but I have not been able to see any versions prior to Huston's entry on the scene.[1] Nevertheless it seems fairly safe to assume that Huston worked directly from the novel, motivated by his longstanding interest in Traven, with whom he shared certain temperamental and intellectual qualities.

By choosing *Treasure* he was returning to the same themes he had explored in *The Maltese Falcon.* Once again he was

1. See, for example, David Thomson's *A Biographical Dictionary of Film* (New York: William Morrow, 1976), p. 497.

adapting a tough, "masculine" novel about a group of characters in search of a treasure; once again the search ends in
ironic failure—indeed, Walter Huston's burst of Homeric
laughter at the conclusion (see figure 24) has the same function as Sydney Greenstreet's philosophic chuckle when he discovers that the black bird is made of lead; once again the
quest for riches enables the director to depict a paradoxical
blend of human greed, ingenuity, and resilience; and once
again the behavior of a small, eccentric group at the margin of
ordinary society becomes the vehicle for a satire of the whole
culture.

That satire, moreover, has a distinctly leftist quality. By
selecting Dashiell Hammett and B. Traven as the basis of his
first two films, Huston was indirectly declaring his sympathy
with the ethos of Popular Front literature in the 1930s; hence
the special appeal of his early pictures lay not merely in their
gritty, anti-Hollywood "realism" and in the cleverness of their
acting ensembles, but in the slightly muffled, allegorical criticism of social life in America that they derived from their
sources. For example, as Steven Marcus has observed in an
essay on Dashiell Hammett, the Maltese Falcon acts as a sym-
bol for the history of capitalism and capitalist culture: "It is
originally a piece of plunder, part of what Marx called 'primitive accumulation'; when its gold encrusted with gems is
painted over, it becomes a mystified object, a commodity. . . .
At the same time it is another fiction, a representation or
work of art—which turns out itself to be a fake."[2] The falcon
also enables Hammett to show what Marcus calls a "pre-
Marxist" or Hobbesian view of human relations, based on
universal warfare and instinctive mistrust. Thus the thieves
who search for the falcon are in direct competition with one
another—like parody capitalists—and Sam Spade's cool head,
natural suspiciousness, and practical ethics are the only things
that save him from a folly like theirs.

In the case of B. Traven, whose Marxist ideas were more

2. Steven Marcus, Introduction to *The Continental Op* by Dashiell Hammett
(New York: Random House, 1974), p. xxv.

conscious and more foregrounded than Hammett's, the argument is similar: The treasure in the mountains has behind it a long history of colonial, Roman Catholic, and capitalist exploitation of Mexico. Of little utility in itself, the gold becomes a commodity used for filling teeth or for decoration—in the words of one of the prospectors, the nuggets are "just crying to you to take them out of the ground and make them shine in coins and on the fingers and necks of swell dames" (scene 15). When the plunder accumulates, however, it provokes a basic mistrust. "As long as there's no find," the character Howard says, "the noble brotherhood will last, but when the piles begin to grow, that's when the trouble starts" (scene 13). As Traven himself puts it, once the gold is collected, its owners have "left the proletarian class and neared that of the property-holders." They have "reached the first step by which man becomes the slave of his property."

The "Mystery" of Traven

Huston was such an admirer of Traven's work that he became involved in correspondence with the author during the early drafts of the screenplay—a communication facilitated by Paul Kohner, the literary agent in California for both men. Traven had earlier written a complete, unproduced film script based on his book *The Bridge in the Jungle* and was, according to Huston, prone to "digress and go into the philosophy of the camera."[3]

Like nearly everyone who had managed to correspond with the man, Huston became curious about the so-called mystery of Traven, who had become as secretive and jealous of his true identity as have writers like Salinger and Pynchon in our own day, and nearly as paranoid as some of the characters in his novels. Little was known about him, except that he was a

3. Gerald Pratley, *The Cinema of John Huston* (South Brunswick and New York: A. S. Barnes, 1977), p. 59. For further discussion of Traven and the film, see Stuart Kaminsky's *John Huston, Maker of Magic* (New York: Houghton Mifflin, 1978).

best-selling writer in Europe and Latin America, ar
claimed to be a forty-seven-year-old U.S. citizen li
recluse in Mexico. He never even revealed what the I
his first name stood for, and he wrote angry letters ro Paul
Kohner when the Warner Brothers contracts identified him as
"Bruno Traven."

Ultimately, after their long communication about the movie
script, Huston arranged a meeting with Traven in Mexico
City. In an interview with Gerald Pratley, he tells this curious
story of what transpired:

> I was in my hotel room in Mexico City and I awoke early in the
> morning. I'm one of those people who never locks his door wherever
> he is. Standing at the foot of my bed was the shadowy figure of a
> man. He took a card out and gave it to me. I put on the light, it was
> still dark, and it said, "Hal Croves, Interpreter, Acapulco and San
> Antonio." I said, "How do you do, Mr. Croves." Then he said, "I
> have a letter for you from Mr. B. Traven," and he gave me the letter,
> which I read. It said that he himself was unable to appear but this
> man knew as much about his work as he himself did and knew as
> much about the circumstances and the country and he would repre-
> sent Traven in every way. We had conversations, Croves and I, for
> the few days I was in Mexico City. I gave him the script, he read it,
> liked what he read and said he was sure Traven would like it very
> much.[4]

Naturally Huston suspected at first that Hal Croves was
Traven incognito, but he was never able to find out for certain. He hired Croves as technical adviser while the movie
company was on location in Mexico, and when the film was
released *Life* magazine ran an article comparing a candid
photo of Croves on the set with another photo purporting to
be a 1927 likeness of Traven. Humphrey Bogart was asked to
identify the man in the older picture. "Sure, pal," the *Life*
reporter quoted him as saying, "I'd know him anywhere. I
worked with him for ten weeks in Mexico."[5] Huston, however, was less certain, because he thought the personality of

4. Pratley, *The Cinema of John Huston*, p. 59.
5. *Life*, February 12, 1948, p. 36.

Croves was inconsistent with the "generous" man he had known through the letters. "To this day I have my doubts," he told Pratley, and the doubts will probably remain because Croves, who in later years allowed himself to be called Traven, is now dead.[6]

Adapting the Novel to a Screenplay

Whatever assistance Huston received from Traven/Croves, *The Treasure of the Sierra Madre* was a slightly more difficult book to adapt for movies than *The Maltese Falcon* had been. With Hammett's short novel, which was already cast in dramatic form, Huston had made few changes, preserving the dialogue almost verbatim. Traven, however, used the adventure of the three prospectors as a starting point for a series of digressions, giving the reader several minor stories related to the central one. These secondary stories, which are narrated by the characters in the main plot, create a history of Mexican society and an atmosphere of economic determinism, making the three prospectors only the latest agents in a very old process. For example, Howard tells about the legendary Aqua Verde mine, which had been discovered and worked by the ancient Aztecs. He describes the Spanish conquistadors as greedy sadists who tortured the Indian miners Inquisition-style, holding out crucifixes before their victims and giving part of the treasure to the Holy Father in Rome. Indian villages were raided to work the mine, until the Indians took revenge and massacred everyone in sight, covering over the mine entrance and leaving it hidden. Then a party of Americans rediscovered the treasure in 1900, but fell out among themselves. One of the survivors of this expedition was subsequently persuaded to try to find the mine again; when he was unable to locate the spot he was tortured by his suspicious companions, and when he returned home to Kansas his house was burned down by angry, greedy neighbors.

Huston compared Traven's digressive technique to Melville,

6. Pratley, *The Cinema of John Huston*, p. 61.

and remarked that "Traven was not a man who reduced his material to the bare essentials, the bone structure, but he was always putting on flesh."[7] Huston's first job, therefore, was to strip away the secondary stories, reducing the novel to the short fable that lay at its heart. As a result, his script gains over the novel in intensity and dramatic unity, but it lacks the historical background and Traven's vigorously anticlerical, anticapitalist commentary. Because of some small structural changes, it also increases the sense of doom that presides over the prospecting expedition. The bandit Gold Hat, for instance, appears only once in the novel, in a digression about a horrifying train robbery told by Lacaud (or Cody, as Huston calls him). In the film, the prospectors themselves experience an attempted train robbery, and Gold Hat appears every time they see bandits. First Dobbs tries to shoot him from a train window, but a jolt causes him to miss; later, when a band of desperadoes invades the mining camp, Dobbs fires a warning shot straight into their leader's yellow sombrero; finally, having stolen his partners' goods, Dobbs encounters Gold Hat a third and fatal time, the bandit having become his nemesis. The film is therefore heavy with coincidence, and it uses a more obvious symbolism than Traven had intended.

Hollywood-Style Elements

Although Huston was dealing with a left-wing novel, which he seems to have genuinely admired, he was willing at various points to add material in keeping with a traditional Hollywood mythology. For example, he makes Curtin (Tim Holt) the most boyish of the three prospectors and has him tell about his plans to use his share of the gold to buy land and raise peaches, an ambition that contrasts sharply with Dobbs's vision of expensive haberdashers, "swell cafes," and sexy dames. At one point in the film, Curtin rests beside the campfire and recalls what life was like in the orchards of his youth:

7. Pratley, *The Cinema of John Huston*, p. 60.

One summer when I was a kid I worked as a picker in a peach harvest in the San Joaquin Valley. It sure was something. Hundreds of people—old and young—whole families working together. After the day's work we used to build big bonfires and sit around 'em and sing to guitar music, till morning sometimes. You'd go to sleep, wake up and sing, and go to sleep again. Everybody had a wonderful time . . . (scene 47)

This speech, backed by Max Steiner's lush music, creates a vision of contented labor that is actually at odds with Traven's writing. On the other hand, it conforms nicely to a pastoral, puritan theme that in Hollywood is at least as old as D. W. Griffith; the most decent of the characters has been given a rustic dream involving family life, whereas Dobbs, the most untrustworthy of the group, has a libidinous yearning for big cities and flashy women.

In a similar vein, Huston has invented the sentimental episode involving the death of Cody, the fourth prospector who walks into the mining camp just before the bandit attack. In the novel, this character is not at all interested in sharing the other men's discovery; instead he wants to work nearby, in a separate mine, because he is convinced that a richer lode lies undiscovered somewhere in the mountain. He helps the other three ward off a bandit attack, as in the film, but then he goes off to prospect alone. He is still working when the original three leave with their riches, and Howard cites him as an example of what he calls an "eternal prospector":

He can stay for ten years at the same place digging and digging, convinced that he is on the right spot . . . He is sure that some day he will make the big hit . . . I really feel sorry for that guy. . . . But you can't cure these fellers, and I suppose if somebody could cure them they wouldn't like it. They prefer to stay this way. It's their whole excuse for being alive.[8]

Huston, like Traven, makes Cody a driven man with the

8. B. Traven, *The Treasure of the Sierra Madre* (New York: Alfred A. Knopf, 1935), p. 214.

slightly haunted look of a compulsive gambler, but he uses the character for purposes different from Traven's. Cody's death helps make the terror of the bandits seem more real; in addition, it provides an opportunity for Curtin to read aloud the letter that is discovered on the dead man's body. This letter has no counterpart in Traven, being comparable to nothing so much as a device frequently used in Hollywood movies about World War II. (Alan Dwan's *The Sands of Iwo Jima* is perhaps the most notable example, but see also David Miller's *Flying Tigers*; for a noncombat movie in the same period that uses the same sort of dead-man's letter, see William Wellman's *The Ox-Bow Incident*.) "Little Jimmy is fine," Cody's wife says, "but he misses his daddy almost as much as I do. . . . I've never thought any material treasure, no matter how great, is worth the pain of these long separations" (scene 102). The difference from the typical war film, of course, is that here the letter acts as a criticism of the men's struggle rather than as a validation of it. In the best Hollywood tradition, it evokes a loving wife and family, a warm hearth left behind, and it suggests that money can't buy happiness. Significantly, Curtin reads a passage in the letter which seems to have been written for his ears alone: "The country is especially lovely this year. It's been a perfect spring—warm rains, hardly any frost. The upper orchard looks aflame and the lower like after a snow storm. Everybody looks forward to big crops. I do hope you are back for the harvest" (scene 102).

B. Traven had never suggested, as the reading of this letter does, that the three prospectors ought to be at home rather than out prospecting; indeed, he never suggested that they *could* be doing something else. Traven's itinerant laborers are in Mexico to find work, and failing that they try their hands at prospecting. Like most laboring men, they are materialists pure and simple, without the luxury of an idealism that comes with all the comforts of home. Huston, however, has contrasted the search for gold with a supposed "real" treasure, exemplified in the movie by the natives who adopt Howard as a medicine man, and by the vision of ripe orchards in Texas.

In other words, just beneath the surface of this hard-boiled movie about desperate work and the failed dream of riches, he has inserted a rather complacent morality, turning the story farther away from a satirical history of capitalism and closer to a generalized critique of materialism. Even the end of his film is slightly less sardonic and satirical than his source, providing a sort of poetic justice for the three main characters: Dobbs, the greedy and psychopathic member of the group, ends up being murdered by bandits; Howard, the wisest and eldest, becomes a healer and demigod for a society of agricultural Indians; and Curtin is last seen bound for Texas, where he might meet Cody's widow and settle down to an idyllic life among the fruit trees.

Huston (or perhaps his producers at Warners) has also softened the political impact of the story by cutting several touchy speeches, drawn mainly from Traven, that were at first intended to be used in the film. For example, an early version of the script had Dobbs and Curtin overhear two men talking about hard times in Mexico: "I'll tell you why the boom's over," one of the men says. "The Mexican government's going to declare all oil lands the property of the nation." In the final revised shooting script, published here, this reference to U.S. exploitation of Mexican resources is even more explicit and is linked to the story of the prospectors, giving Howard an opportunity to voice Traven's theories of social determinism. Dobbs remarks that the Mexican bandits "don't know what mercy is," and Howard replies:

Know why? Because they've never been shown any. If our people in the States had lived in poverty under all sorts of tyrannies for hundreds of years they'd have bred a race of bandits too, every bit as cruel and bloodthirsty. Come right down to it we are bandits of a kind. What right have we got to go looting their mountain anyway? About as much right as the foreign companies that take their oil without paying for it . . . and their silver and their copper. (scene 96)

In the film, this speech has been dropped. Also omitted is an earlier exchange of dialogue that uses the gold hunt to illustrate a simple theory of economics. As the three men begin to divide their gold, Dobbs complains that he should have a larger share because he put up most of the money for the expedition. "In civilized places the biggest investor always gets the biggest return," he says. "That's one thing in favor of the wilds," Howard comments, and then goes on:

I think you're wise not to put things on a strictly money basis, partner. Curtin might take it into his head he was a capitalist instead of a guy with a shovel and just sit back and take things easy and let you and me do all the work. He'd stand to realize a tidy sum on his investment without so much as turning his hand over. If anybody's to get more, I reckon it ought to be the one who does the most work. (scene 47)

In the film, Dobbs complains that his share ought to be bigger, but Howard's comparison of capitalism and socialism has been cut, allowing the audience to draw their own conclusions.

Elements Atypical of Hollywood

All this, however, is not to say that *The Treasure of the Sierra Madre* is a purely orthodox film. Huston's ending is close enough to what Traven had written, and the picture as a whole is one of the most resolutely unglamorous features ever to be produced by a Hollywood studio. It has practically no sex, no expressionist charm, and none of the *nostalgie de la boue* that had made *The Maltese Falcon* such a romantic pleasure to watch.

Treasure is the story of gold before it has been mystified into objects, before it has been transported into the world of the film noir, and before it has provoked the more subtle villainies of urban civilization. It is one of the few forties movies about hard labor, its most "civilized" moment occurring when two of the characters order expensive whiskey in a Mexican dive. And for a movie that takes place outdoors, it has an oddly claustrophobic effect; there is not a single attempt to compose an attractive landscape for the camera, the major part of the story being told through close-ups of sweaty, unshaven faces.

As in *Falcon*, Huston seems more interested in the physiognomy of his players and in tight, three-figure compositions than in the environment itself (see, for example, figures 6, 11, 13, and 22). One occasionally glimpses a wide vista, but only when it is absolutely necessary to the narrative, as when the three prospectors look down from their mountain and make out a group of bandits moving toward them across a scrubby desert. Half of the action is shot at night, around a tiny, studio-manufactured campsite, and in daylight there is nothing to look at but rocks, cactus plants, and a lonely gila monster. Even the gold isn't pretty—in fact, much to the surprise of Dobbs and Curtin, in its natural state it has the color of mud.

The film is all the more unusual because it cannot be fit into any of the familiar Hollywood genres. Indeed, Warners' advertising campaign is fascinating to contemplate because all its publicity schemes, which are based on standard marketing procedures, stand in ironic relationship to the actual picture. Theater posters featured an artist's rendering of the three leading players, behind them a montage of colorful scenes purporting to be from the movie: a band of sombreroed horsemen at full gallop, their leader astride a white charger; a handsome, mustachioed rider in the act of rescuing, or perhaps capturing, a dark-haired, big-breasted woman in a low-cut blouse. The ads vaguely suggest a western, except that Bogart wears a fedora instead of a cowboy hat, and he scowls out at the viewer like Duke Mantee.

The theme of treasure was, of course, strongly emphasized in all the publicity campaigns, exhibitors being advised to promote the picture through newspaper contests and "treasure hunts" for free passes. The Warners press book even suggested that theater owners could visit local banks and negotiate a display of bullion or gold coins—in other words, the studio was trying to lure audiences into the theaters by means of the very greed that the film had satirized.

Introduction

Dobbs (Humphrey Bogart)

Humphrey Bogart was also one of Warners' major selling points; in fact, he was *Treasure*'s only major star, and without his strong backing Huston might never have been able to make the picture at all.[9] In the "tie-up" ads used to promote the opening of the film, he was featured in various store window displays endorsing a line of men's clothing; an assortment of slickly lit photos showed him modeling topcoats, sport shirts, tuxedos, hats, and pipes—all the farthest cry from the attire of Fred C. Dobbs.

The trouble was that, as the insecure and ultimately paranoid prospector who deserts one of his companions and almost murders the other, Bogart had given the studio very little material for attractive publicity; indeed, he had returned to the sort of part he was identified with in the thirties, when he was usually cast as a cowardly heavy. His acting recalls *Black Legion* (1936), in particular, where he appeared as a working-class family man, frustrated and envious of his fellow workers, who joins a Klan-style organization in order to live out his fantasies of power. Dobbs's inauthentic swagger, his sour discontent, and his almost childlike conversations with himself all seem to derive from this pathetic, obsessive character, who had been one of Bogart's most effective if least appealing roles.

But then Bogart's screen persona had always suggested the possibility that the Dobbs in him might surface at any moment. As a leading player after 1941, the year Huston helped make him a star in *The Maltese Falcon*, he usually appeared in two different guises that stood in mirror-image relation to one another. One was the heroic figure of *Casablanca* and *Key Largo*—an idealist turned momentarily cynical, an embittered loner cultivating his selfish instincts, who ends up sacrificing his own interests for the good of a community. The other was the unstable character in *Treasure* and later in *The Caine Mutiny*, a Nixonesque fellow who was generated by an exact reversal of the heroic pattern—outwardly a dedicated member

9. See James Agee, *Agee on Film*, vol. 1 (New York: McDowell Obolensky, 1958), p. 399.

of a community, a would-be idealist, he ultimately betrays the group out of selfishness, fear, and neurosis. Both character types were potentially sociopathic, but in his heroic appearances Bogart overcame anger and isolation, while in his more villainous or untrustworthy roles he was overcome by them.

As Dobbs, Bogart is quite good at suggesting the desperation and bitterness of a man who has no job and whose hard luck is at least partly the result of his own instability. In fact, he is so unstable that James Agee described him as a distracting, potentially weak element in the story. "It is impossible to demonstrate or even to hint at the real depth of the problem, with him on hand," Agee wrote in his admiring review of the film for *The Nation*. "It is too easy to feel that if only a reasonably restrained and unsuspicious man were in his place, everything would be all right; we wouldn't even have wars."[10]

To Bogart's credit, however, it should be noted that both he and Huston tried to make the character into as much a victim as a villain. The entire opening section of the film is devoted to him, showing the brutal determinants of his psychology and the humiliations of his typical day. He eyes a cigarette butt in the street, but loses it to a Mexican boy who struts offscreen puffing smoke and holding his head cocked high (see figure 1). Several times he panhandles money from an American in a white suit, but he is so ashamed of what he is doing that he cannot look his mark in the eye and doesn't realize that he is repeatedly approaching the same man (a cameo played by John Huston himself—see figure 2). First he uses the money for food and smokes, and in a cafe he encounters a ragged Mexican boy (Robert Blake) who tries to sell him lottery tickets. Irritable and resentful that Mexican children have any kind of work when he doesn't, he tosses a glass of water in the boy's face; but when the boy stands there and persists with the sales talk, he relieves his guilt by buying a ticket. Later he bums enough money for a shave and a haircut, emerging with comically greased-down hair and powdered cheeks (see figure 3). Strolling down the street out-

10. Agee, *Agee on Film*, p. 293.

side, he eyes a prostitute (figure 4) and bums more money, this time being told by the man in the white suit to "go occasionally elsewhere." Dobbs's constant need of cash in these scenes, and the resentment and pressure he feels without it, are a prelude to his difficulties in the remainder of the film, where his emotional state can be seen swinging instantaneously from friendliness to distrust, from braggadocio to fear, from optimism to despair. He is always on the edge of something, and Bogart's brittle, even fragile physique and rather wild eyes suggest that he might break down at any moment.

Whatever the moral failings of this character, we are at least persuaded that such men exist; furthermore, Huston has tried to preserve and amplify Traven's notion that there is nothing special about him, that there is a bit of Dobbs in us all. Howard, who is clearly the mouthpiece for the author, repeatedly emphasizes that when money is at stake no one is to be trusted, and in an early episode of the movie we see his maxim illustrated when Dobbs and Curtin are hoodwinked by their employer, whom they are forced to fight for their wages. It is a grotesque, dirty battle, initiated when the burly, straw-hatted boss (Barton MacLane) smashes Curtin on the head with a whiskey bottle and punches Dobbs to the floor, kicking him in the face (see figure 7). The two smaller men keep stumbling back into the fight, grabbing at the boss's heels and swinging often enough to start connecting, until they begin wearing their opponent down (see figure 8) and at last empty his wallet. Later, when Dobbs wins money from the lottery and joins forces with Curtin and Howard on the gold hunt, he tries to assert his superiority over this dog-eat-dog behavior, making a huge display of comradeship: "So put 'er there . . . partner," he says to Curtin. As the two shake hands, the camera closes in on Howard, looking up at Dobbs with the knowledge of what gold can do to brotherly feeling (see figure 10).

After the gold has been discovered in the mountains, Huston adds a scene that is not in the novel, emphasizing the temptation confronting all three men: Dobbs is working in a mineshaft when a roof collapses; Curtin sees that his partner is trapped, but he hesitates for a moment before his better instincts prompt him to dig Dobbs out. His brief hesitation, incidentally, is not mentioned in the final script and is apparently one of Huston's revisions during the actual filming of the picture. We are supposed to recall this scene when, toward the end of the movie, Curtin denounces Dobbs for shooting him and leaving him to die. Huston gives Howard the last word: "I reckon we can't blame him too much. . . . I mean he's not a real killer as killers go. I think he's as honest as the next fellow—or almost. The mistake was in leaving you two alone in the depths of the wilderness with more'n a hundred thousand between you. . . . I'd have been tempted too" (scene 123).

This belief in the pervasiveness of greed is ironically confirmed by the scene in which the bandits kill Dobbs. There are three bandits, just as there have been three prospectors, and the quarrel over the dead man's belongings serves to parody the action of the film as a whole: "Give me that shoe, you dirty cheat," one bandit cries in Spanish as he strips the body. "It's mine. I saw them first." "What difference is it to me who went for them first?" asks the other bandit. "I threw the stone that laid him out." Once again the acquisition of property turns men into enemies, and once again bickering over who deserves what share of the goods leads to trouble—as the bandits argue among themselves, Dobbs's pack mules almost escape.

Howard (Walter Huston)

As Howard, the grizzly prospector who does most of the talking and carries the burden of the film's message, Walter Huston has an acting problem that is in one sense the opposite of Bogart's: He has to make the character seem authentic and believable while being always right about everything. If Dobbs is "fantastically undisciplined and troublesome,"[11] as Agee contended, then Howard is in danger of seeming impossibly

11. Agee, *Agee on Film*, p. 293.

wise and windy. John Huston seems to have recognized this problem, because in the early drafts of the script he marked several of Howard's speeches with the marginal notation "too long." Nevertheless, most of these speeches have been retained, and Walter Huston has dealt with them by removing his false teeth and speaking with extreme speed through his nose. Some of his longer monologues are thrown away so rapidly that it takes a couple of viewings of the film to hear them properly, but despite this underplaying he becomes the most interesting presence in the movie—a smart, spry, unpretentious old geezer whose performance is all the more remarkable considering that it could easily have degenerated into a Gabby Hayes sort of cuteness.

And although Howard is supposed to be a disarmingly wise, honest fellow, he has a rather clever theatrical sense that suggests another, perhaps more human side to his character; notice, for example, the way he gathers an audience in the Oso Negro flophouse with his tales of gold, or the way he "cures" an Indian child who has nearly drowned. John Huston has staged this latter scene in an area that resembles a Greek theater, a dramatically lit stage surrounded by ranks of Indian men and women shown in Eisensteinian montage. When Howard lifts the child in his toughened old hands, which are his most expressive feature, it is easy to see how the Indians could worship and adopt him as their medicine man (see figures 14–16). In the equivalent scene in the novel, Traven comments that Howard "admitted to himself that the boy if left entirely alone might, perhaps, have come to just as well," and in the film it becomes clear that the old prospector enjoys his pretense of power. His reward—and it is surely the most one could expect, even with piles of gold—is shown by a few witty, idyllic images: We see him reclining on a hammock, cooled by shade trees, while behind him naked children dive and splash in a forest pool. He munches a watermelon, spitting the seeds into a girl's hand, and takes a sip of tequila. The natives bring him gifts, including a caged bird and a squealing baby pig. A pretty girl lights his cigarette and rubs his beard affectionately (see figures 18–20). He therefore becomes an almost perfect early version of *The Man Who Would Be King*, except that his pleasure in being worshiped by the Indians is never allowed to develop into tragic hubris.

Other Roles

The minor roles in the film are also vividly and skillfully portrayed, even if they make up an improbable, neatly contrasting set of types. At one point Warners intended to cast Burgess Meredith and Ronald Reagan as Curtin and Cody, but Tim Holt and Bruce Bennett are probably better choices, the one suggesting a burly farm boy and the other a likeable, intelligent, but obsessed man with tragic undertones to his character.

Of all these secondary players, however, Alfonso Bedoya is the most important. A virtual amateur when the film was made, he has an awkwardness that gives a feeling of documentary authenticity to the Gold Hat figure, who has a simple-minded, childlike cunning and a tendency to switch suddenly from a con man's charm to a primal ruthlessness. Precisely because he is in one sense a bad actor, Bedoya always lets us know that he might drop his grin at any moment, revealing violence underneath a pretended calm. Huston reportedly coached him very little, leaving him confused and insecure, but this anxiety has helped make him all the more contradictory and frightening a personality; the expression on his chubby, slightly grotesque face never quite matches his nervous eyes, and the tone of his speech is alternately fawning, honey-sweet, and psychotic. All of his close-ups are eloquent. Consider, for example, the low-angle shot of him when he discovers Dobbs alone and unprotected near a water hole, a sleepy smile spreading across his face and light filtering through the holes in his sombrero like flashing gold (see figure 21). Later, when the Federales toss him in jail prior to his execution, he tries to snarl and spit through the bars of his prison, but his eyes seem as dazed and fearful as a maddened animal (see figure 23).

Introduction

Huston the Director

By all accounts, Huston's method of dealing with most of his actors is casual and nondirective. He is brilliant at the art of casting (Audie Murphy as the boy soldier in *The Red Badge of Courage*, Sterling Hayden and Louis Calhern as a safe-cracker and his fence in *The Asphalt Jungle*, everybody in *The Maltese Falcon*), and when he has done a good enough job of choosing the players, the characterizations seem to evolve without much intervention. He often lets the actors block their own movements, finding that they instinctively make logical and expressive patterns as they rehearse; in fact, one of the pleasures of watching his movies comes from the body language of the people on the screen, who often form little tableaux, always telegraphing their function by the way they move, stand, or sit. Thus James Agee was fascinated with the way the three prospectors in *Treasure* behave when they discover the body of Cody after the bandit attack (see figure 13):

Bogart, the would-be tough guy, cocks one foot up on a rock and tries to look at the corpse as casually as if it were fresh-killed game. Tim Holt, the essentially decent young man, comes past behind him and, innocent and unaware of it, clasps his hands as he looks down, in the respectful manner of a boy who used to go to church. Walter Huston, the experienced old man, steps quietly behind both, leans to the dead man as professionally as a doctor to a patient and gently rifles him for papers. [12]

There are other examples of this largely improvised choreography throughout the film, as when Cody first walks into the campsite: Bruce Bennett has a calm but slightly weary intensity, squatting on his haunches in an unthreatening position that allows freedom of movement should any trouble develop; Tim Holt and Walter Huston sit by the campfire, Huston facing the newcomer, his hands on show, affecting total casualness; meanwhile Bogart paces nervously in a semicircle just outside the group, uncertain what to do but hankering after violence. The most effective instance of the method

12. Agee, *Agee on Film*, p. 329.

comes near the end, in the wonderfully frightening scene when the three bandits discover Bogart alone with the gold. While Bedoya questions Bogart, the other two killers look him up and down, scurrying about like curious monkeys. One of them puts on Bogart's hat and lifts his pants leg to examine his shoes; the other slides rump first down a slope in the ground, stopping at his quarry's feet and sitting there, looking up and waiting for the kill (see figure 22).

Although Huston is generally regarded as an unobtrusive, almost styleless director, images like these show that he has a fondness for formal, sometimes rather static groupings that create simple visual statements; the groupings may have been achieved naturally, without his coaching, but they arise inevitably out of the kinds of stories he likes to tell, which are moral fables with clearly defined functions for the characters. In keeping with such stories, his camera usually acts as a quiet bystander, listening to the story rather than telling it. He says that he thinks of the camera as "another actor on the set," but this actor, at least in *Treasure*, is more of an observer than an agent of the action, more of an auditor than a narrator. Throughout the film, Huston's technique might be described as the art of knowing when to move in and overhear important dialogue, and when to sit back and watch a figure cross the screen. Frequently he shows violent action obliquely, as when the Mexican bandits are hidden from view by a wall when they line up before a firing squad. It is a mistake, however, to regard all this self-effacing style as "invisible," because it has a studied casualness and a clearly expressive purpose.

As a result, the visual quality Huston puts on the screen is recognizably his own, not simply the unmanipulated appearance of actual life. The special look of his films seems to me to come from his fondness for authentic locales, offbeat and unglamorous faces, and rather tightly composed shots of heads and bodies in conversation. Hence Ted McCord's sharp, deep-focus photography in *Treasure* is seldom used to create dynamic spaces or long takes; Huston is more interested in slightly documentary-style close-ups that record the lines on an actor's face or the tatters in a costume. He evokes a Mexican town, a sleepy cantina, and an Indian village without using complex establishing shots or sweeping camera movements, relying instead on natural lighting, true locations, and carefully selected extras to give believability to his images. Despite the conservative way he shoots and edits, there remains in his work an unusually strong ethnographic quality, putting him more in the tradition of Flaherty and the neo-realists than in the line of classic Hollywood directors. Although some of his best films (*The Maltese Falcon, The Asphalt Jungle*) have been made completely inside a studio, he seems most himself when he stages his films in some primitive or exotic spot, and he is probably as responsible as anyone for Hollywood's postwar movement away from back-lot settings.

The sense of a particular time and place in *Treasure* struck many of the contemporary reviewers as the film's most conspicuous virtue. Bosley Crowther's review in *The New York Times* said that Huston had "resolutely applied the same sort of ruthless realism that was evident in his documentaries of war."[13] James Agee, who wrote the best-known and most intelligent accounts of the film for *Time, Life,* and *The Nation,* repeatedly stressed the unaffected, natural artistry of McCord's camera and the truthfulness of the settings. At the other extreme were the trade journals like *Daily Variety,* which tried to assess the picture according to its box-office potential, ultimately categorizing it in generic terms as "action stuff with heavy masculine appeal."

In retrospect, the truth about the film seems to lie somewhere between these opposing views. *Treasure* is unorthodox by some standards, traditional by others. Huston is a director who finds expressive, sometimes even Hollywoodish material outside the studio, in real places; despite the relaxed air he assumes on the set and in interviews, he can hardly be called a pure "realist" (whatever one chooses to make that overused term signify). He is in fact a somewhat didactic film maker whose films are stamped consistently with his own personal-

13. Bosley Crowther, review in *New York Times,* January 24, 1948, p. 11.

ity. Within the limits of his taste and technique he can be a powerfully effective artist, and he is certainly a true *auteur*.

Many of the strengths of Huston's best work—unpretentious intelligence, economy, witty observation of a basically cruel society—can be seen in the following screenplay. One needs, of course, to watch the finished film in order to appreciate him fully, but more than some Hollywood directors he is a man whose particular talents are rooted in his scripts. To read him here is to understand how good he can be when he has respect for his source, a reluctance to compromise too much, and the same mixture of luck, courage, and tenacity that can be found in his most memorable characters.

My thanks to Rudy Behlmer for answering questions about production of the film and to Lee Sterrenberg for talking with me about Traven's work.

1. Dobbs (Humphrey Bogart) loses a cigarette butt to a Mexican boy, who picks it off a Tampico street.

2. An American in a white suit (John Huston) scowls at Dobbs before giving him money.

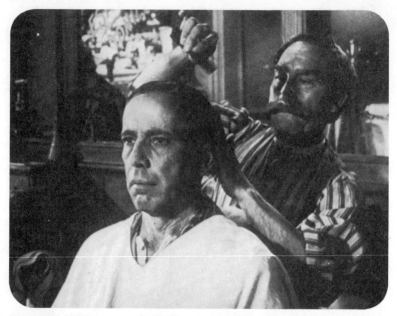

3. *Dobbs visits a barber.*

4. *After his haircut, Dobbs eyes a prostitute.*

5. Curtin (Tim Holt) and Dobbs at work in an oil field.

6. After a day of drinking beer and waiting for their wages, Dobbs and Curtin encounter Howard (Walter Huston) in the Oso Negro flophouse.

7. *Pat McCormick (Barton MacLane) tries to beat up Dobbs and Curtin, who have cornered him in a bar and demanded their wages.*

8. *Dobbs and Curtin slowly wear McCormick down as the fight proceeds.*

9. At the Oso Negro, Howard tells stories of gold.

10. Howard looks doubtfully up at Dobbs, who shakes hands with Curtin and calls him "partner."

11. The three prospectors divide their gold dust.

12. Curtin saves Dobbs when the mine caves in.

13. *Dobbs, Curtin, and Howard discover the dead Cody.*

14. *Howard gives artificial respiration to an Indian child.*

15. *A group of Indians look on as Howard works.*

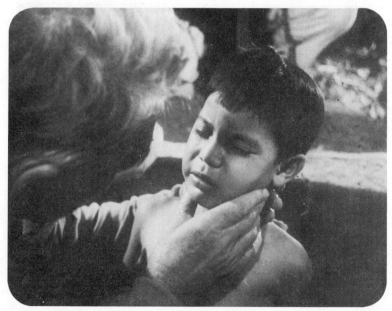

16. *Howard lifts the child, who begins to come back to life.*

17. Dobbs takes Curtin's gun and prepares to kill him.

18. Howard lives like a king among the Indians.

19. He dines on watermelon.

20. A pretty girl attends him.

21. *Gold Hat (Alfonso Bedoya) discovers Dobbs alone at a water hole.*

22. *The bandits gather round Dobbs, waiting to kill him.*

23. *Gold Hat in jail.*

24. *Howard roars with laughter when he discovers that the gold has been blown away by the wind.*

The Treasure of the Sierra Madre

Screenplay

by

JOHN HUSTON

From the novel

by

B. Traven

The Treasure of the Sierra Madre

Locale: Mexico

FADE IN

1. CLOSE-UP LOTTERY LIST

showing the winning numbers drawn in the MEXICAN NATIONAL LOTTERY. AUGUST 5, 1924. CAMERA PULLS BACK to include Dobbs. He is slowly tearing a lottery ticket into bits. CAMERA DOLLIES AHEAD of him as he turns away from the list. The tribes of bootblacks that people the streets do not pester Dobbs. He is too obviously on his uppers. His clothes are ragged and dirty and his shoes are broken. He hasn't had a haircut in months, and there is several days' growth of beard on his face. He stops a passing American.

DOBBS:
Can you spare a dime, brother?[1]

The American growls, moves on. Dobbs turns, looks after the departing figure. The American flips a cigarette away. Dobbs's eyes follow its flight.

2. CLOSE-UP THE BURNING CIGARETTE

in the gutter.

3. CLOSE SHOT DOBBS

He moves half a step toward the gutter, then halts and looks right and left to make sure no one is watching. This brief delay costs him the cigarette. One of the swarm of bootblacks swoops down on it. Dobbs pulls his belt in a couple of notches and continues on up the street. CAMERA DOLLIES AHEAD. Something Dobbs sees OUT OF SCENE causes him to increase his

47

pace. He catches up with an American who is dressed in a white suit.

DOBBS:

Brother, can you spare a dime?

White Suit fishes in his pocket, takes out a tostón, and gives it to Dobbs who is so surprised by this act of generosity that he doesn't even say thanks. For several moments he stands rooted, looking at the coin in his palm. Then he closes his hand around it, making a fist. Putting the fist in his pocket, he cuts across the street. CAMERA PANS with him to a tobacco stand where he stops to buy a package of cigarettes, then hurries along. CAMERA PANS him to a sidewalk restaurant.

DISSOLVE TO:

4.   EXT. SIDEWALK RESTAURANT
Dobbs at a table. He has just finished eating. The proprietor is serving him with coffee.

DOBBS:

How much?

PROPRIETOR:

Treinta centavos.

Dobbs pays with a tostón. Then he takes a black papered cigarette out of the newly purchased pack, lights up, and sits back to smoke and enjoy his coffee. A little boy, barefoot, in ragged cotton pants and a torn shirt, enters through the open door of the restaurant brandishing lottery tickets.

BOY:

Michoacan State Lottery, señor.

DOBBS:

Beat it. I'm not buying any lottery tickets. Go on, beat it.

BOY:

> Four thousand pesos the big prize. (He pulls at Dobbs's coat sleeve.)

DOBBS:

> Get away from me, you little beggar.

BOY:

> The whole ticket is only four pesos, señor. And it's a sure winner.

DOBBS:

> I haven't got four pesos.

BOY:

> Buy a quarter of a ticket for one peso silver. (He pulls at Dobbs's pants leg.)

DOBBS (picks up water glass):

> If you don't get away from me I'll throw this right in your face.

BOY (not moving):

> Then one tenth of a ticket, señor, for forty centavos.

Dobbs throws the water into the boy's face. The boy laughs, wipes the water off with his sleeve. The proprietor comes back with the change. Dobbs tips him cinco centavos. The proprietor goes back behind his counter.

BOY (eyes on the change):

> Señor ought to buy one twentieth. One twentieth costs you only twenty centavos. Look, señor, add the figures up. You get thirteen. What better number could you buy? It's a sure winner.

Dobbs weighs the coin in his hand.

DOBBS:

> How soon is the drawing?

BOY:
> Only three weeks off.

DOBBS:
> All right. Give me the twentieth so I don't have
> to look at your ugly face any longer.

The little merchant tears off the twentieth of the sheet,
hands it to Dobbs in exchange for a silver coin.

BOY:
> It's un numero excelente, señor. (Bites on coin to
> see if it's good.) Muchas gracias, señor. Come
> again next time. I always have the winners, all
> the lucky numbers. Buena suerte, good luck!

Off he hops, like a young rabbit, after another pro-
spective customer. Dobbs finishes his coffee, pushes
back his chair, and rises. He lets his belt out three
notches.

5. EXT. RESTAURANT
CAMERA PANS with Dobbs across the street to the plaza
where he sits down on one of the benches beside
another man. He takes out his cigarettes, puts a new
one in his mouth, and lights it from the old. A
bootblack picks up the end he throws away.

DOBBS (to his companion on the bench):
> Cigarette? (He extends the pack.)

The man takes one. Dobbs gives him a light with his
own.

CURTIN:
> Thanks.

Curtin takes a long drag, inhales deeply, then blows
smoke out of his mouth and nose. He looks to be
in his late twenties—about ten years younger than
Dobbs. He has a strong, hard-bitten face with a
slightly crooked nose. Like Dobbs, he could use a
haircut.

DOBBS:
Hot.

CURTIN:
Yeah.

DOBBS:
Some town Tampico.

CURTIN:
You said it, brother. If I could just land me a job that'd bring in enough so's I could buy me a ticket I'd shake its dust off my feet soon enough you bet.

DOBBS:
I beat my way up El Higo last week. There ain't a camp where any work's to be had. I tried 'em all.

CURTIN:
You're telling me . . . more companies are closing down all the time. Guys I've known who've worked steady for the past five years are coming back from the fields to town. Why? I don't savvy. The world needs oil . . .[2]

A man in a white suit passes the bench. Dobbs's eyes follow him speculatively.

DOBBS:
If I was a Mex I'd buy a can of shoe polish and go into business. They'd never let a gringo. You can sit on a bench three-quarters starved. You can beg from another gringo. You can even commit burglary. But try shining shoes in the street or selling lemonade out of a bucket and your hash is settled. You'd never get another job from a white man.[3]

CURTIN:
Yeah, and the natives would hound and pester you to death.

DOBBS (getting to his feet):
It's a hell of a country to be broke in.

CURTIN:
Tell me the country that isn't.

Dobbs turns away from the bench.

6.   CLOSE SHOT   SHOESHINE STAND
The man in the white suit is reading a paper while he gets a shine. Dobbs ENTERS SCENE.

DOBBS:
Brother, can you spare a dime?

White Suit takes a tostón out of his pocket, gives it to Dobbs. For the second time this day, Dobbs is surprised into speechlessness. He looks up from the coin in his palm to the white-suited man on the wire bootblack stand. The latter's face is hidden by the newspaper. Dobbs thrusts the coin into his pants pocket, turns on his heel, and marches off.

7.   EXT. OPEN-AIR BARBER SHOP   CLOSE SHOT   DOBBS
in barber chair. Laying aside his razor, the barber pushes a handle and Dobbs's position changes from horizontal to sitting. A mirror is put into Dobbs's hand. He holds it at various angles, studying the effects of the scissors on the back of his head.

BARBER:
¿Algo en el pelo, señor? Para que quede bonito.
(He shows Dobbs a bottle.)

DOBBS:
¿Cuánto vale?

BARBER:
Quince centavos.

Dobbs frowns slightly, debating with himself whether to indulge in this extravagance.

BARBER:

Muy bonito aroma.[4]

DOBBS:

Okay.

The barber douses his head liberally, then he combs Dobbs's hair. Dobbs uses the hand mirror again, the results being much to his liking. His head shines like a nigger's heel. Having performed the final rite of snipping the scissors below each of his customer's nostrils, the barber unfastens the sheet from around Dobbs's neck. Dobbs rises from the chair and gives the barber his one and only tostón. He continues to eye himself while the barber makes change, and it must be that he receives an excellent impression, for he is more than liberal when it comes to tipping.

BARBER:

Gracias, señor. Come again.

Dobbs issues forth into the street. The change in his manner is rather more noticeable than the change in his appearance. His shoulders are back as he walks, his glance bolder. He allows it to fall on a passing damsel whose swarthiness cannot be hidden by the layers of powder on her face. Returning Dobbs's look, her eyes show interest, but this fades as she gives him the once-over and sees the condition of his clothes. Dobbs turns to watch her retreating figure. The girl goes into a two-story house, on the front of which is a sign in Spanish:

CUARTOS AMUEBLADOS[5]

He tosses the last remaining piece of change out of the tostón in his hand. Alas, it is far too little. Returning it to his pocket, he sighs and continues on down the street. Reaching the corner, he observes a man in a white suit about to step off the curb. Dobbs goes directly up to him.

DOBBS (to the white suit):
> Can you spare a dime, mister?

White Suit reaches in his pocket, takes out a tostón. Dobbs reaches for it. But White Suit keeps the piece between his fingers.

WHITE SUIT:
> Listen, you. Such impudence never came my way as long as I can remember.

Dobbs stands utterly perplexed while the stranger continues.

WHITE SUIT:
> Early this afternoon I gave you a tostón. When I was having my shoes polished I gave you another tostón. Now, once again. Do me a favor, will you? Go occasionally to somebody else. This is beginning to get tiresome.

DOBBS:
> Excuse me, mister. I never realized that it was you all the time. I never looked at your face, only your hands and at the money you gave me. Beg pardon, mister. I promise you I won't put the bite on you again.

WHITE SUIT:
> This is the last you get from me, understand? (Gives Dobbs the tostón.)

DOBBS:
> Sure, mister—never again will I—

WHITE SUIT:
> Just to make sure you won't forget your promise, here's another tostón so you'll eat tomorrow.

DOBBS (taking it):
> Thanks, mister, thanks.

WHITE SUIT:
> But understand—from now on you are to try your

best to make your way in life without my assistance.

And the gentleman goes his way. Dobbs clinks the
two tostóns together thoughtfully, then turns on his
heel and starts rapidly up the street he just came
down.

8.   EXT. WATERFRONT   OPPOSITE FERRY LANDING   DUSK
CAMERA DOLLIES with Dobbs as he walks slowly along,
his eyes on the pavement. He stops outside a cantina,
listening to the tinny music of a player piano. The
swinging door opens and two sailors come out.

DOBBS:
    Brother, can you spare . . . ?

They push past him and are gone. He is about to start
on when the door opens a second time and a man,
very tall and bulky, appears.

DOBBS:
    Can you spare a dime, brother?

McCORMICK (interrupting):
    I won't give you a red cent, but if you want to
    make some money I'll give you a job.

DOBBS:
    What's the catch?

McCORMICK:
    No catch. I got a job for you if you want it. Hard
    work but good pay. Ever rig a camp?

DOBBS:
    Sure.

McCORMICK:
    The ferry's making off and one of my men hasn't
    shown up. I don't know what's happened to him.
    He's probably filthy drunk in some dive.

DOBBS:
What's the pay?

McCORMICK:
Eight bucks, American, a day. Grub goes off on your expenses . . . Well, don't just stand there. Make up your mind. You have to come the way you are. No time to get your clothes or anything. The ferry doesn't wait.

DOBBS:
I'm your man.

The huge fellow takes Dobbs by the arm. CAMERA PANS as he hurries him across the street toward the ferry landing.

9. ABOUT A DOZEN MEN
standing in the semidarkness. McCormick and Dobbs ENTER SCENE. McCormick starts counting heads. Dobbs recognizes one of the gang as the man with whom he had conversation on the bench during the morning.

DOBBS:
Hello.

CURTIN:
Hello yourself.

McCORMICK;
Okay, you guys, get aboard.

They move to obey.

DISSOLVE TO:

10. EXT. A CLEARING IN THE JUNGLE
About fifty men are at work rigging a camp, amongst them Dobbs and Curtin. They are engaged in the erection of a derrick. Dobbs, one leg snake-fashion around a cable, grabs the heavy boards that are swung up, and bolts them. Curtin helps to bring the boards into position. Sweat is pouring off them. From time to

time they groan under their exertions. OVER SCENE a voice: "Come and get it." Dobbs and Curtin pull themselves up, straddle a wooden girder, and wipe the sweat out of their eyes. Then, hand over hand, they slide down the cable. They start over to where a line of men is forming. McCormick falls into step with them.

McCORMICK:

What's the matter? Can't you two take it?

DOBBS:

Must be a hundred and thirty in the shade and there ain't any shade up on the derrick.

McCORMICK:

What the devil. Just figure you're a couple of millionaires in your own private steambath. The sooner we're through the sooner we'll be back in town drinking cold beer. (He lowers his voice confidentially.) If we finish within two weeks I'm going to give you fellows a bonus.

DOBBS:

It's coming to us, working sixteen, eighteen hours a day like we do.

McCORMICK:

Now don't start crying for your mothers. What do you want? I'm paying top salaries . . . and a bonus.

DOBBS:

What about our pay anyway? And when do we get it? I haven't seen a single buck out of you yet, Pat.

McCORMICK:

You'll get your dough all right. Don't you worry about that . . . When we get back to Tampico. What would you do with money here anyway except gamble and lose it. You'll get paid as we step off the ferry . . .

DISSOLVE TO:

11.   EXT. WATERFRONT FERRY LANDING IN BACKGROUND
Little groups of men, members of McCormick's work gang, are standing around. McCormick comes up to one such group, which includes Curtin and Dobbs.

DOBBS:

> What's up, Pat? We were to get our money as we stepped off the ferry.

McCORMICK:

> The agent was supposed to be here with it. I don't know what could have happened. Nothing to worry about, though. I'll go over to the office and pick it up myself. (Pulls Dobbs aside—lowers his voice.) Supposing I meet you two in about an hour at that cantina right off the Plaza.

DOBBS:

> Any objection to us going along with you?

McCORMICK (suddenly angry):

> What's the matter, don't you trust me? Do you think I'd run out on you?

DOBBS:

> No, Pat, I don't think you'd do a thing like that, but I haven't got a cent, even to buy me a new shirt, or one glass of beer.

McCORMICK (takes some money out of his pocket):
> Here's ten pesos. That ought to hold you for an hour. (He takes his watch out.) It's a quarter to two. I'll be at that cantina no later than three o'clock.

He turns and goes abruptly off before there can be any further objections.

DISSOLVE TO:

58

12. CLOCK OVER CANTINA BAR
It says 5:30.[6]

BARTENDER'S VOICE (OVER SCENE):
> Pat McCormick, sí. He comes in here time to
> time. No see him lately.

CAMERA PULLS BACK to include Dobbs, Curtin, the bartender, and one other customer.

CUSTOMER (ruggedly built, middle-aged man, slightly
drunk):
> Pat McCormick? What about Pat McCormick?

DOBBS:
> He was supposed to meet us here.

CUSTOMER:
> Does he owe you any money?

Dobbs nods.

CUSTOMER:
> How long you guys been around Tampico any-
> way?

Curtin and Dobbs cock their heads at the other man.
Scowls appear on their faces.

DOBBS:
> What's that got to do with it?

CUSTOMER:
> Only foreigners and half-baked Americans fall for
> Pat McCormick's tricks.

CURTIN:
> How do you mean?

CUSTOMER:
> I mean he gets dumb guys like you to work for
> him, and when the time comes for him to pay off,
> he takes a powder. (He throws back his head and
> laughs.)

Curtin and Dobbs scowl at each other. Then they look at their beer. Curtin murmurs something under his breath that is probably unprintable, then:

CURTIN:

> How much we got left out of the ten he gave us, Dobbsie?

Dobbs takes money out of his pocket, counts it.

DOBBS:

> Six-fifty.

CURTIN:

> Not even enough for one bed.

DOBBS:

> I know a joint where we can get cots for fifty centavos a night. It's full of rats and scorpions and cockroaches, but beggars can't be choosers.

> > DISSOLVE TO:

13. INT. OSO NEGRO SLEEPING QUARTERS
CAMERA DOLLIES AHEAD of Dobbs and Curtin as they move down the narrow aisle between two rows of cots on which men are sitting or lying. We OVERHEAR scraps of conversations.

FIRST MAN:

> I been in on half a dozen oil booms. It's always the same story. One day the price per barrel goes down two bits. Nobody knows why. It just does. And the next day it's down another two bits. And so on until, after a couple of weeks, jobs that were a dime a dozen ain't to be had, and the streets are full of guys pushing each other for a meal.[7]

Dobbs and Curtin have found their cots by this time and have begun to undress. Another conversation is taking place in the far corner of the room among three Americans. One, an elderly fellow whose hair is beginning to show white, is lying on his cot. The other two sit, half undressed, on their cots.

HOWARD (the old man):

Gold in Mexico? Sure there is. Not ten days from here by rail and pack train, a mountain's waiting for the right guy to come along, discover her treasure, and then tickle her until she lets him have it. The question is, are you the right guy . . . ? Real bonanzas are few and far between and they take a lot of finding. Answer me this one, will you? Why's gold worth some twenty bucks per ounce?

MAN (after a pause):

Because it's scarce . . .

Dobbs and Curtin, undressing, listen to the old man.

HOWARD:

A thousand men, say, go searching for gold. After six months one of 'em is lucky—one out of the thousand. His find represents not only his own labor but that of the nine hundred ninety-nine others to boot. Six thousand months or fifty [*sic*] years of scrabbling over mountains, going hungry and thirsty. An ounce of gold, mister, is worth what it is because of the human labor that went into the finding and the getting of it.

MAN:

Never thought of it just like that . . .

HOWARD:

There's no other explanation, mister. In itself, gold ain't good for anything much except to make jewelry and gold teeth.

They are silent for a while thinking their thoughts. The old man rolls a cigarette and lights it. Then he resumes:

HOWARD:

> Gold's a devilish sort of thing anyway. (He has a faraway look in his eye.) When you go out you tell yourself, "I'll be satisfied with twenty-five thousand handsome smackers worth of it, so help me Lord and cross my heart." Fine resolution. After months of sweating yourself dizzy and growing short on provisions and finding nothing, you come down to twenty thousand and then fifteen, until finally you say, "Lord, let me find just five thousand dollars worth and I'll never ask anything more of you the rest of my life."

FIRST MAN:

> Five thousand's a helluva lot.

HOWARD:

> Here in the Oso Negro it seems like a lot. But I tell you, if you were to make a real find, you couldn't be dragged away.

Dobbs and Curtin have stopped undressing to listen to what the old man is saying.

HOWARD:

> Not even the threat of miserable death would stop you from trying to add ten thousand more. And when you'd reach twenty-five, you'd want to make it fifty, and at fifty, a hundred—and so on. Like at roulette . . . just one more turn . . . always one more. You lose your sense of values and your character changes entirely. Your soul stops being the same as it was before.

DOBBS (unable to restrain himself):

> It wouldn't be like that with me. I swear it. I'd take only as much as I set out to get, even if there was still half a million bucks worth lying around howling to be picked up.

Howard looks at him, examining, it seems, every line in his face. The scrutiny goes on for some time; then he shifts his eyes away and continues as though he had not been interrupted.

HOWARD:

I've dug in Alaska, and in Canada and Colorado. I was in the crowd in British Honduras where I made my boat fare back home and almost enough over to cure me of a fever I'd caught. I've dug in California and Australia . . . all over this world practically, and I know what gold does to men's souls.

SECOND MAN:

You talk like you struck it rich some time or other. How about it, Pop, did you?

The faraway look comes back in Howard's eyes, and he nods.

SECOND MAN:

Then how come you're sitting here in this joint—a down-and-outer?

HOWARD:

Gold, my young man. That's what it makes of us. Never knew a prospector that died rich. If he makes a fortune, he's sure to blow it in trying to find another. I ain't no exception to that rule. (He shakes himself as though to throw off past memories.) Sure, I'm an old gnawed bone now, but don't you kids think the spirit is gone. I'm all set to shoulder a pickax and shovel again any time somebody's willing to share expenses. I'd rather go all by myself. That's the best way . . . going it alone. Of course, you've got to have the stomach for loneliness. Lots of guys go nutty with it. On the other hand, going with a partner or two is dangerous. All the time murder's lurking about. Hardly a day passes without quarrels—the partners accusing each other of all sorts of crimes, and suspecting whatever you do or say. As long as there's no find, the noble brotherhood will last, but when the piles begin to grow, that's when the trouble starts.

CURTIN:

Me, now, I wouldn't mind a little of that kind of trouble.

FIRST MAN:
Me neither, brother!

DOBBS:

Think I'll go to sleep and dream about piles of gold getting bigger and bigger . . .

Howard reaches out, turns off the kerosene lamp.

DISSOLVE TO:

14.   EXT. PLAZA CLOSE SHOT CURTIN AND DOBBS AFTERNOON on the bench where first they met. It is obvious by their appearance that no luck has come their way.

DOBBS:

Do you believe what that old man who was doing all the talking in the Oso Negro the other night said about gold changing a man's soul so's he ain't the same person he was before finding it?

CURTIN (after a moment, thoughtfully):
Guess that depends on the man.

DOBBS:

Exactly what I say. Gold don't carry any curse with it. It all depends on whether or not the guy who finds it is a right guy.

Curtin's eyes are caught and held by something OUT OF SCENE. He is no longer listening to Dobbs.

64

DOBBS (continuing):
The way I see it, gold can be as much of a blessing as a curse.

CURTIN:
Hey, Dobbsie!

DOBBS:
Yeah?

CURTIN:
Look at who's coming out of the Hotel Bris-
tol . . . Is that Pat McCormick or am I seeing
things?

DOBBS:
It's him!

CUT to include McCormick as he strolls in the direction
of the Plaza. A Mexican dame by his side is flashing a
low-cut dress, a silk parasol, and considerable phony
jewelry.

CURTIN:
Let's get him. Let's get him hard.

McCormick stops in his tracks as the two rush toward
him.

McCORMICK (grinning):
Hello, boys. How are you? Want a drink?

His extreme affability has the effect of keeping the two
men from sailing right into him. He addresses the
dame.

McCORMICK:
Perdoni Shlucksy dear, mi vida, I've got some
business to attend to with these two gentlemen.
You go back into the hotel and wait. I won't be
long.

He steers her back toward the hotel.

McCORMICK:
Unos minutos no más, Chiquita.

She disappears into the lobby. He faces Dobbs and Curtin.

McCORMICK:
Let's have a drink. It's on me.

DOBBS:
Okay.

They step into a cantina.

McCORMICK (to the bartender):
Three shots of rye.

CURTIN:
Make mine brandy, 3 Star.

DOBBS:
Two brandies.

McCORMICK:
Rye is good enough for me.

The drinks are put down before them.

McCORMICK:
Well, boys, I suppose you're wondering about that money that's coming to you. Fact is I haven't been paid on that contract yet myself. If I had the money, you'd get it first thing. You know that. I'll take you both on my next contract. It'll go through by Monday and we can set out Friday. Glad to have you boys with me again. Well, here's mud in your eyes.

They all drink.

CURTIN:
We want what's coming to us, and we want it right here and now.

McCORMICK:

Didn't I just get through telling you—

CURTIN:

Better come across, Pat.

McCORMICK:

Tell you what I'll do, boys—I'll give you twenty-five percent—oh, I reckon I can make it thirty. The balance, let's say, the middle of next week.

CURTIN:

Nothing doing. Here and now. Every cent you owe us or I swear you won't walk out of here. You'll have to be carried.

McCORMICK:

Now let's not stop being friends. How about another drink? (To the bartender.) Two more Hennesseys for these gentlemen. Put the bottle on the bar.

DOBBS:

If you've got any ideas about getting us liquored up—

McCORMICK:

I'm only inviting you to have a friendly drink with me!

He reaches for the bottle. Instead of pouring, he hits Curtin on the head with it. Curtin goes down. McCormick swings at Dobbs. Dobbs ducks, then backs away. McCormick starts after him but Curtin, on the floor, grabs him around the knees. McCormick tries to kick himself free but Curtin hangs on. Now Dobbs plants his fist squarely in the big fellow's face. It's a long fight and a tough one. At times it's Dobbs who's down and Curtin who's up. They fight in relays, one carrying on while the other gets over the effects of his punishment. Were it not for their determination, born of hunger, Dobbs and Curtin would surely be the losers. But finally the huge hulk of McCormick collapses and goes down, not to get up again. His eyes are both swollen shut and his face is a misshapen pulp.

McCORMICK (begging):
I'm licked . . . I'm licked.

CURTIN:
Give us our money.

DOBBS:
Yeah, give us our money.

They rain kicks on him while he feels blindly for his back pocket, produces his wallet.

McCORMICK:
I can't see . . .

Dobbs takes money from the wallet, counts out what's coming to himself and Curtin. Then he throws a bill to the bartender.

DOBBS (to the bartender):
For the use of your cantina. (To Curtin.) Come on. Let's beat it before the law arrives.

They stumble out through the rear door.

LAP DISSOLVE TO:

15.   WATER FOUNTAIN
SHOOTING at the reflections of the two men in the water. They are bathing their wounds.

DOBBS:
You know something, Curt?

CURTIN:
What?

DOBBS:
We ain't very smart if we hang around Tampico waiting for a job. Our money'll get shorter every day until we're right back where we were—on the

bum again, pushing guys for dimes and sleeping in freight cars and what have you.

CAMERA PULLS BACK to CLOSE SHOT of Dobbs and Curtin.

CURTIN:

That's right. Got any ideas?

DOBBS:

Yeah. That old man in the Oso Negro started me thinking.

CURTIN:

What about?

DOBBS:

Why not try gold digging for a change? It's no riskier than waiting round here for another break. And this is the country where the nuggets of gold are just crying to you to take them out of the ground and make them shine in coins and on the fingers and necks of swell dames.

CURTIN (catching Dobbs's enthusiasm):

One thing, living is cheaper in the open than it is here in Tampico. Our money would last longer, and the longer it lasts the greater our chance of digging up something would be.

DOBBS:

We'd have to have equipment, of course . . . picks and spades and pans and burros. Wonder how much it would all cost?

CURTIN:

The old man would know.

DOBBS:

The sooner we leave the better. When we're on our way it'll be like investing our money. That old man could give us some pointers all right. He's too old to take along, of course. We'd have to carry him on our backs.

CURTIN:

> You can't tell about some of these old guys. It's surprising sometimes how tough they are . . . I don't know what gold looks like in the ground. I've only seen it in shop windows and in people's mouths. Do you know anything about prospecting?

DOBBS:

> Not much, come right down to it.

CURTIN:

> We might have real use for an experienced guy like that old-timer.

DOBBS:

> Maybe you're right. Let's go hunt him up right away.

DISSOLVE TO:

16.   INT. OSO NEGRO   DOBBS, CURTIN, AND THE OLD MAN ARE IN A HUDDLE

HOWARD:

> Will I go? What a question. Course I'll go. Any time, any day. I was only waiting for one or two guys to ask me. Out for gold? Always at your service. (He takes a pencil and begins scribbling on the back of a magazine.) I've got three hundred American bucks ready cash here in the bank. Two hundred of them I'm all set to invest. It's the last money I have in the world. After it's gone I'm finished up. But, if you don't take a risk you can't make a win. How much dough have you guys got to put in?

DOBBS:

> I got a hundred and fifty bucks and Curtin here has the same.

A little boy, barefoot and ragged, is moving down the aisle by the rows of cots, brandishing lottery tickets.

BOY:

> Buy a ticket on Loteria National—one hundred thousand pesos—the big prize.

HOWARD:

> Five hundred bucks—that ain't hardly enough to buy tools and weapons and the most essential provisions.

DOBBS:

> Weapons? What do we need weapons for?

HOWARD:

> Meat's one thing. We'll kill our own. And bandits is another . . . We ought to have anyway six hundred bucks between us.

DOBBS:

> That much, eh?

HOWARD:

> Can't you dig up any more?

DOBBS:

> Not a red cent.

17.   INT. OSO NEGRO   ANOTHER ANGLE

A few feet away from the three men, the boy selling lottery tickets stops in his tracks and stares intently at Dobbs, then he rushes forward.

BOY:

> Give me my money, señor—ten percent I get for having sold you the prize-winning ticket.[8]

DOBBS (misunderstanding):

> Get away from me.

BOY:

Please señor—it is the custom. Whoever draws the lucky number always gives a present to the seller of the ticket. If you don't do it you will have bad luck for the rest of your life. (He takes hold of Dobbs's coat.)

DOBBS:

I tell you I don't want any lottery ticket. (Suddenly hearing the kid.) What? What's that—?

HOWARD:

He says you bought a winning ticket from him.

A memory flashes through Dobbs's mind. He leans forward, peers into the boy's face, then he begins to dig and claw in his watch pocket. He produces a lottery ticket, unfolds it, and holds it toward the boy.

DOBBS:

Here—is this what you mean?

BOY:

Sí, señor, sí . . .

DOBBS:

You say it's a winner?

BOY (in Spanish):

Sí, señor—a two hundred peso prize. (He sorts through the sheets of winning numbers, finds the date he is looking for, and holds it out for Dobbs to see.) Three—seven—two—one.

DOBBS (shouts):

My number!

CURTIN:

Sure enough.

DOBBS:

Just look at that fat, rich, printed number! Two hundred pesos! That's the sugar Papa likes. Welcome, sweet little smackers. (He takes a bill out of his pocket.) Here's your present, sonny boy, with my blessing.

BOY (all smiles now):
Muchas gracias, señor. (He exits on the run.)

18.   CLOSER SHOT   DOBBS AND CURTIN

DOBBS (extends his hand to Curtin):
You want to shake the hand that bought this ticket?

Curtin takes Dobbs by the hand.

CURTIN:
Congratulations.

DOBBS (pumping Curtin's hand):
Congratulations yourself. You stand to profit by this same as I do.

CURTIN:
How do you make that out?

DOBBS:
Didn't the old man say we needed six hundred—and that's how much we got now, isn't it? (He kisses the ticket.)

CURTIN:
Yeah . . . but . . .

DOBBS:
But what?

CURTIN:
Why should you be putting up for me?

DOBBS:
This is an all or nothing proposition. If we make a find we'll be lighting our cigars with hundred dollar bills. And if we don't, the difference between what I'm putting up and you're putting up ain't enough to keep me from being right back where I

73

was half an hour ago, polishing a bench with the seat of my pants. (Once more he holds his hand out.) So put 'er there . . . partner.

FADE OUT

FADE IN

19.   EXT. LONG MOVING SHOT
the arid mountains of Durango. CAMERA PULLS BACK TO:

20.   INT. DAY COACH
crowded with Indians and mestizos. CAMERA MOVES UP the aisle to a CLOSE SHOT of Dobbs, Howard, and Curtin. Dobbs is asleep. Howard and Curtin are peering at a map the old man is holding on his knees. Howard is drawing on the map—lines and dots over small sections.

HOWARD:
We'll buy our burros at Perla and head northeast away from the railroad. It's no use looking anywhere nearby a railroad or any kind of a road at all, because construction engineers make it their business to examine every bit of ground around the roads while they're building them. We have to go where there's no trail—where you can be positive no surveyor or anybody who knows anything about prospecting has ever been before. The best places are those where anybody who's on salary wouldn't go because he wouldn't think it worth his while to risk his hide.

All of a sudden the brakes of the train are applied, so violently that people are flung out of their seats. Scarcely have they picked themselves up than they are knocked down again. The car wheels scream on the rails. The train stops and a babble of voices begins.

VOICES:
¿Qué pasó? Parece que chocó el tren.

74

OVER SCENE comes the SOUND of scattered firing.

VOICES:
No es un choque. Son bandidos. Están asaltando el tren.

A number of the women and some of the men begin to pray. Howard makes a grab for his gun, and Dobbs and Curtin follow suit.

HOWARD (shouts):
Echense al piso, pronto. De barriga, ándenle.[9]

The natives in the car do as he bids. Almost immediately bullets begin to hit the side of the coach and sing through its windows.

CUT TO:

21.   EXT. TRAIN   LONG SHOT   SHOOTING THROUGH WINDOW
The area is strewn with boulders, and from behind those near the tracks little puffs of smoke are rising. The partners fire their revolvers whenever they see a sombrero.

All at once the bandits are up, racing toward the train. The three partners fire steadily through the train windows and several of the bandits go down. A few reach the coach and are killed or wounded while trying to enter. That the attack will be a failure is apparent almost as soon as it begins. Before they have covered half the distance, most of the bandits are hugging the ground or seeking cover.

And now the train jolts into motion again. Some horsemen COME INTO VIEW. All but one are dismounted, firing over their saddles. Three horses have been hit and are down. The mounted bandit is wearing a hat painted with gilt that mirrors the sun. He sits boldly upright, firing his rifle from the shoulder. At the moment when our coach is directly opposite him, he spurs his horse and gallops alongside the train, firing away. After a hundred yards or so the train, gathering speed, leaves him behind. . . . No more bullets are hitting the coach. Presently the sound of firing ceases. People start getting to their feet. It seems nobody has been seriously hurt, at least in this coach. Bullet holes are inspected and commented upon with gusto. The danger through which they have passed serves to unite the passengers and make them all one family. The men slap each other's backs. A bottle of moscal starts making the rounds. Everybody is talking at once.

DOBBS:

I got three of 'em. You can credit me with three. (To Curtin.) How many did you get?

CURTIN:

A couple I guess.

DOBBS:

I'm one up on you, Curtin. (To Howard.) Bet you didn't get as many as I did, Pop. I got three. Good shooting, eh? (He points to a groove on the side of the window from which he was firing.) Hey, look! One hit right by my ear not two inches away. Close.

CURTIN:

The bullets were sure coming thick and fast. For a minute it was like a swarm of bees in this coach.

DOBBS:

That bandit in the gold hat who rode his horse alongside the train—I had my sights on him nice as you please, but the train gave a jolt and I missed, dammit. Sure wish I'd got him.

A passenger comes in from the next coach and repeats, so everyone can hear, information relayed back from the head of the train:

PASSENGER:

Pusieron una piedra en la vía. Se pegaron chasco

los bandidos, porque vienen tropas adelante y atrás. Hubo pocos muertos a bordo. (In English for Dobbs's and Curtin's benefit.) There was a big boulder on the track put there by bandits—that's why the train stop. When bandits board they got big surprise. Soldiers on the train, front and rear, and they were waiting for them. Not many passengers got killed.

Howard has picked the map up from the floor and sat down with it, spreading it across his knees. Out comes his pencil again.

HOWARD (as though nothing of moment had happened):
Here's where we're bound for—hereabouts. I can't make out properly on this map whether it's mountain, swamp, desert, or what, but that shows the makers of the map themselves don't know for sure. Once on the spot all we have to do is wipe our eyes and look round us. Yeah, and blow our noses. Believe it or not, I knew a feller once could smell gold just like a jackass can smell water.

DISSOLVE TO:

22. INT. GENERAL STORE   DOBBS, HOWARD, CURTIN, STOREKEEPER

Staple groceries and merchandise are on the shelves lining the walls. Various articles of merchandise hang from the ceiling—pack saddles, rope, etc. Through the open doorway a pile of boxes can be glimpsed—the equipment that came by train with the three partners. Howard, his map out, is leaning on the counter conversing in Spanish with the Storekeeper, a tall, elderly man with graying hair and bronzed face. Curtin stands a little way off, trying to follow what is being said. Dobbs roams around the store trying on articles of apparel.

STOREKEEPER:

A cinco días hay un río. Muy caudaloso en el ve-
rano, pero seco en el invierno.

Howard draws the river on the map.

STOREKEEPER (continuing):

Más allá hay montañas muy altas, más que las
nubes. Terreno peligroso. Hay que abrirse paso a
machete y hay muchos reptiles y insectos de pi-
cada mortal. También hay tigres muy feroces que
pueden arrastrar a un burro y hasta subirlo a un
arbol.

Dobbs brings items he has selected from the stock—a
belt with a fancy buckle, a pair of half boots, and a
wide brim felt hat—over to the counter, puts them
down. The Storekeeper reckons their value on his fingers.

DOBBS:

Getting any dope?

HOWARD:

Five days from here there's a river. It's dry in the
winter. Beyond that river the country's very wild
and dangerous. Mountains rise above the clouds
and we must cut our way through the valleys
which are full of deadly insects and huge snakes,
and ferocious tigers so big and strong they can
climb trees with burros in their mouths . . .

A boy enters.

HOWARD (continues):

Good . . . ! I'm pleased to hear tall tales about
where we're going, because it means mighty few
outsiders have set foot there.

BOY:

Aquí está mi primo con unos burros. ¿Quieren
verlos?

HOWARD (to Dobbs and Curtin):
There's some burros outside for us to see.

PAN with them to the door, beyond which a number of burros are standing.

DISSOLVE TO:

23. EXT. MOUNTAINS LONG SHOT
of the three men and their burros—tiny moving specks in the distance.

DISSOLVE TO:

24. MED. SHOT HOWARD CLIMBING A STEEP SLOPE
The old man proceeds at the unwearying gait of one who's accustomed to measuring out endless miles with his legs.

25. DOBBS AND CURTIN
They are fairly staggering with weariness. Dobbs half falls, half sits down, gropes blindly for his canteen, opens it. He raises the canteen, takes a mouthful of water, spits it out, then drinks along.

DOBBS:
> If there is any gold in those mountains, how long will it have been there?

CURTIN:
> Huh?

DOBBS:
> Millions and millions of years, won't it . . . ? So what's our hurry. A couple of days more or less ain't going to make much difference.

CURTIN:
> Remember what you said back in Tampico about having to carry the old man on our backs—

DOBBS:
> That's when I took him for an ordinary human being and not the son of a goat. Look at him climb, will you?

26.   LONG SHOT   HOWARD
moving unwearyingly up the steep slope.

CURTIN (grinning):
> What gets me is how he can go all day long
> under this sun without water.

DOBBS:
> He's part goat I tell you.

CURTIN:
> If I'd only known what it meant to go prospecting
> I'd have stayed right in Tampico and waited for a
> job to turn up . . . What's the matter?

Dobbs is peering at the ground where he splattered
water. Now he goes down on one knee to examine it
more closely.

DOBBS:
> Look! Look how it glitters.

Curtin kneels down beside him.

CURTIN (drawing in his breath):
> Yeah.

DOBBS:
> It's yellow too . . . like . . . like . . .

He's afraid to say the word.

CURTIN:
> . . . like gold.

Dobbs reaches for the canteen, pours more water out
on the ground.

DOBBS:
> It's all around . . . (He pours some water onto a
> rock.) Look, Curtin, here's a vein of it in this
> rock.

They are fairly prancing with excitement now.

CURTIN (cups his hands, calls):
> Howard! Howard, come back here! We've found something.

27. CLOSE SHOT   HOWARD
high above the others on a mountain. He turns at the sound of their voices.

CURTIN'S VOICE (OVER SCENE):
> Come back.

Without hesitation, he starts back down, running when he can.

> CUT BACK TO:

28. CURTIN AND DOBBS

DOBBS:
> What else could it be. Only gold shines and glitters like that. We've struck it, Curtin, or I'm crazy, and from the looks of things we've struck it rich.

CURTIN:
> Looks like it.

Dobbs is splashing more water out of his canteen and exclaiming:

DOBBS:
> Maybe we've found a whaddya call it—a mother lode.

Howard comes trotting up. Dobbs seizes him by the arm.

DOBBS:
> Look, Howard, the ground—it's full of gold, and it's in veins in the rocks.

Howard doesn't even bend over. They wait for him to speak, full of expectancy.

HOWARD (finally):
> This here stuff wouldn't pay you a dinner for a truckload, unless you could dump it right in front of a building under construction. It ain't good for anything but mixing with cement.

There's a long silence.

DOBBS:
> It ain't gold?

HOWARD (shaking his head):
> Nope . . . Not to say there ain't gold hereabout. We've walked over it four or five times. There was a place yesterday looked like rich diggings but water for washing the sand was eleven miles away. Too far. The other times there wasn't enough gold to pay us a good day's wages.

Dobbs wears a forlorn expression. Curtin looks sheepish. Howard inspects the packs on the burros, tightens a couple of hitches.

HOWARD (continuing):
> Next time you strike it rich holler for me before you go splashing water around. Water's precious. Sometimes it can be even more precious than gold. (He cuts a burro across its quarters with a willow switch.) Get up.

The pack train starts moving.

DISSOLVE TO:

29. SMALL CAMPFIRE   NIGHT
Howard has cooked hardtack in the skillet and is eating. OVER SCENE the yip-yipping of coyotes halts while a wolf gives out with his long-drawn, mournful howl.

HOWARD:
> Hey, you fellers. How about eating!

But neither of the inert bodies lying with their backs

to the fire shows any sign of life. Howard shakes Curtin by the shoulder.

HOWARD:
> How about eating!

CURTIN:
> Don't want to eat . . . want to sleep.

HOWARD:
> Hey! Dobbs!

Dobbs's only answer is a snore. The coyotes start up again. Old Man Howard finishes his piece of hardtack, wipes his mouth, and takes a harmonica out of his pocket. The music he makes is even more lonely sounding than the howling of the coyotes.

> DISSOLVE TO:

29A.   MED. LONG SHOT   BURRO TRAIN AND THREE MEN
As before, the old man is in the lead. They are traveling into different kinds of country now. Low, sandy hills, dotted with cactus. A wind is blowing. Howard stops, holds up his hand, testing the wind for direction. He squints at the horizon, then hurriedly begins to take the packs off the burros. Dobbs and Curtin come up.

DOBBS:
> What's up?

HOWARD:
> A norther, looks like.

CURTIN:
> A norther? What's a norther?

Even as he asks the question a blast of wind starts the desert sands flying.

HOWARD:
> Big winds from the north this time of year. When

they blow hard enough this desert country stands right up on its hind legs.

He pulls his bandana up so it covers his nose and mouth. Dobbs and Curtin do likewise. The figures of men and beasts become vague shapes behind the curtain of flying sand, then they are obscured entirely.

30.   LONG SHOT   WILD, DESOLATE COUNTRY
First we see no sign of life whatever, but presently there's a movement and a stir in the thick underbrush.

31.   MED. SHOT
of the three wielding machetes, trying to open a trail over which the burros, with their heavy loads, may pass. Even the old man is showing wear and tear. His face is scratched, and sweat and blood mingle to form big drops that drop off the end of his nose and chin each time he strikes with his machete. But he at least works his blade to some purpose. The two others strike out aimlessly, their muscles, out of weariness, no longer obedient. Observing their distress, Howard lowers his machete. It is a signal for Curtin and Dobbs to sink groaning to the ground. Howard seizes the moment to take out makings and roll a cigarette. But the other two simply lie gasping for breath. Their eyes have that animal dumbness to them.

HOWARD (lighting his cigarette):
> I reckon there's only a few hundred yards more of this heavy stuff. Pretty soon we ought to be getting up to where it's rocks and nothing else.

Two or three drags finish the cigarette. Howard grinds it out, then raises his machete. Hearing the ring of the steel as the blade strikes, Curtin tries blindly to imitate the old man. He strikes twice, feebly. There is a SOUND from Dobbs. He looks around. Dobbs is crying, adding tears to the mixture of sweat and blood that gets into his eyes and rolls off his chin.

DISSOLVE TO:

32.   A HIGH ROCKY PLACE
far below which flows an unending sea of brush.

DOBBS:

>   You want to know what I'm thinking? I'm thinking we ought to give up—leave the whole outfit —everything behind and go back to civilization.

HOWARD:

>   What's that you say? Go back . . . Well tell my old grandmother I've got two very elegant bedfellows who kick at the first drop of rain and hide in the closet when thunder rumbles. My, my, what great prospectors—two shoe clerks reading in a magazine about prospecting for gold in the land of the midnight sun or south of the border or west of the Rockies or . . .

DOBBS (howling):

>   Shut your trap.

He picks up a rock, waves it, threateningly. Howard begins to dance a goatish kind of jig.

DOBBS (continuing):

>   I'll smash your head flat.

HOWARD (dancing):

>   Throw it, baby, throw it. Go ahead, just do it. You'd never leave this wilderness if you did. Without me you two would die here . . . more miserable than sick rats.

Dobbs takes a step forward, but Curtin restrains him.

CURTIN:

>   Leave the old man alone—can't you see he's nuts.

HOWARD:

> Nuts, eh? (He laughs in a satanical way, kicking a rock in his dance.) Nuts am I. I'll just tell ya something, my two fine bedfellows . . . You're so dumb there's nothing to compare you with. You're dumber than the dumbest jackass. Look at each other . . . you two. Did ya ever see anything like yourselves for being dumb specimens? (He laughs and kicks his heels together.)

Dobbs and Curtin do look at each other, then they look back at Howard. They are puzzled as to whether the old man has really lost his mind.

HOWARD:

> Why you two are so dumb you don't see the riches you're treading on with your own feet.

They don't get Howard's meaning right away. He kicks a stone then picks it up, throws it up, catches it, all in the course of his dance. Dobbs and Curtin look at each other, mouths agape. Suddenly they drop to their knees, start scratching at the rocky earth.

HOWARD:

> Don't expect to find nuggets of molten gold. It's rich but not that rich. It's only heavy dirt and here ain't the place to dig. It comes from somewhere further up. (He points up toward the mountain crest.) Up there's where we have to go . . . up there . . .

CAMERA PANS UP to a high mountain peak, wearing in its majesty a crown of clouds.

DISSOLVE TO:

33.   INSERT: OF A PAN
the water turning in it. CAMERA PULLS BACK to show Howard panning dirt. They are near the crest of the mountain now, at the place Howard pointed to in the previous scene. Dobbs and Curtin look on at what Howard is doing, their faces sober and intent.

DOBBS:

So that's the way the stuff looks, is it . . . not much different from sand . . . plain sand.

HOWARD:

Gold ain't like stones in a riverbed. It don't call out to be picked up. You got to know how to recognize it. And the finding ain't all. Not by a long shot. You got to know how to tickle it so it comes out laughing. (Sifting some dirt through his fingers.) Mighty rich dirt. It'll pay good.

DOBBS:

How good?

HOWARD:

Oh, this dirt ought to run about twenty ounces to the ton.

CURTIN:

At some twenty dollars an ounce . . . !

The old man nods.

DOBBS:

How many tons will we be able to handle a week?

HOWARD:

That depends on how hard we work . . . We better pitch our camp a mile or two away.

DOBBS:

Why, if here is where we're goin' to dig?

HOWARD:

In case anybody happens by we can tell 'em we're hunters and get away with it maybe . . . We'll cut bushes and pile 'em around the mine itself so it can't be spotted from below.

DOBBS:

I'd sure hate to play poker with you, old-timer.

HOWARD:

> Every so often one of us will have to go to the
> nearest village after provisions. Whoever goes
> first ought to go all the time. That way they'll fig-
> ure only one man's up here. If they find out
> there's more than one they're liable to get sus-
> picious. Hunters usually work alone.

CURTIN:

> Wouldn't it be a lot easier to file a claim?

HOWARD:

> Easier, maybe, but not very profitable. It wouldn't
> be no time till an emissary from one of the big
> mining companies turned up with a paper in his
> hand showing we haven't any right to be here.
> (Squatting there, he picks up some of the dirt,
> sifts it through his fingers. Then he grins at
> Dobbs and Curtin.) How does it feel, you fellers,
> to be men of property . . . ?

FADE OUT

FADE IN

33A.   FULL SHOT   WATER WHEEL

A construction designed to draw water from a tank
and, by means of cans and cases, raise it to an upper
tank from whence, upon opening a lock, the water is
to run back down a wooden sluice to the original
tank. The power that turns the wheel is a burro. The
final nail has just been driven and the moment has
arrived when the handiwork of the three partners is to
be tested. Howard harnesses the burro to the wheel
and kicks it in the rear, setting the wheel and system
of tin cans and boxes into motion. Curtin climbs to the
upper tank, pacing himself according to the speed of
the crude machine.

DOBBS (pumps Howard's hand):

> My hat's off to you. From now on it's your show,
> old-timer. Whatever you say goes far as I'm con-
> cerned.

HOWARD:
> The tanks'll leak some at first till the boards swell and close the seams.

DOBBS:
> I sure had some cockeyed ideas about prospecting for gold. It was all in the finding I thought. Once you found it you just picked it up and put it into sacks and carried it to the nearest bank. (He laughs uproariously at his former innocence.)

HOWARD:
> We might burn some lime out of the rocks and build a tank that wouldn't lose a drop of water.

DOBBS (laughing):
> I'd hate to think what would've happened to Curtin and me if we'd gone it alone. Even if we'd found the stuff we wouldn't have known how to get it out.

HOWARD:
> You're learning. Pretty soon I won't be able to tell you anything. You'll know it all.

If there is any irony in Howard's voice it escapes Dobbs.

HOWARD (to Curtin):
> Tank full yet?

CURTIN:
> Right to the top.

HOWARD:
> Then open up the sluice gate.

CURTIN:
> Right.

He obeys and the water starts running down the sluice. Following Howard's lead, Dobbs begins to wash the sand, trying his best to imitate the actions of the old man.

HOWARD:
> Like this—do it.

DOBBS:
> I get it.

Curtin joins them.

DOBBS (to Curtin):
> This is how it's done—see.

CURTIN:
> Yeah—I get it.

34.   INDIVIDUAL CLOSE-UPS OF THE THREE MEN
as they separate the sand from the gold.

35.   TINY FLAKES OF GOLD
as the sand is washed away.

DISSOLVE TO:

36.   CAMP CLOSE-UP OF DOBBS   NIGHT
His eyes, reflecting the light of the campfire, glitter in
their sockets. He leans forward and we see a Mexican
calendar tacked to the wall. Lines have been drawn
across all the dates up to October 21.

37.   CLOSE-UP OF A SCALE
as the proceeds of the day's work are weighed. CAM-
ERA PULLS BACK to a CLOSE SHOT of the three men.
Howard measures dust onto the scale.

CURTIN:
> How much do you figure it is now?

HOWARD:
> Close on to five thousand dollars worth.

DOBBS:
> When're we going to start dividing it?

Howard looks at him keenly.

HOWARD:
> Any time you say.

CURTIN:
> Why divide it at all? I don't see any point. We're all going back together, when the time comes. Why not wait until we get paid for the stuff, then just divide the money?

HOWARD:
> Either way suits me. You fellers decide.

DOBBS:
> I'm for dividing it up as we go along and leaving it up to each man to be responsible for his own goods.

HOWARD:
> I reckon I'd rather have it that way, too. I haven't liked the responsibility of guarding your treasure any too well.

DOBBS:
> Nobody asked you.

HOWARD (smilingly):
> That's right—you never asked me. I only thought I was the most trustworthy among us three.

DOBBS:
> You? How come?

HOWARD:
> I said the most trustworthy. As for being the most honest, no one can say.

DOBBS:
> I don't get you.

HOWARD:
> Well, let's look the thing straight in the face. Suppose you were charged with taking care of the goods. All right, I'm somewhere deep in the

brush one day getting timber and Curtin here is on his way to the village for provisions. That'd be your big chance to pack up and leave us in the cold.

DOBBS:

Only a guy that's a thief at heart would think me likely to do a thing like that!

HOWARD:

Right now it wouldn't be worthwhile. But when our pile has grown to let's say three hundred ounces think of such things, you will . . .

CURTIN:

How's about yourself?

HOWARD:

I'm not quick on my feet any longer. You fellers are a lot tougher than when we started out. And by the time the pile is big enough to be really tempting I won't be able to run half as fast as either one of you. You'd get me by the collar and string me up in no time. And that's why I think I'm the most trustworthy in this outfit.

Curtin grins.

CURTIN:

Looking at it that way I guess you're right. But perhaps it would be better to cut the proceeds three ways every night. It'd relieve you of a responsibility you don't like.

HOWARD:

Swell by me. After we've gotten more than a couple hundred ounces it'll be a nuisance to carry it around in little bags hanging from our necks, so each of us will have to hide his share of the treasure from the other two. And having done so he'll have to be forever on the watch in case his hiding place is discovered.

DOBBS:
What a dirty filthy mind you have.

HOWARD:
Not dirty, baby. No, not dirty. Only I know what sort of ideas even supposedly decent people can get in their heads when gold's at stake.

DISSOLVE TO:

38.   FULL SHOT   OF THE MINE
There are two tunnels now into the rocky shoulder. OVER SCENE the SOUND of picks. CAMERA MOVES into the interior of one of the tunnels. Howard puts down his pick, starts shoveling the rocky debris out of the cave into the open. CAMERA MOVES to the opening of the other tunnel. Dobbs, some twenty feet in, is swinging away with his pick.

39.   A CRACK IN THE CEILING
of the tunnel over Dobbs's head.

40.   DOBBS'S PICK BITING INTO THE ROCK
OVER SCENE we hear Dobbs's voice.

DOBBS'S VOICE (he grunts):
Whew! Hot! Geez . . . hot.

CUT BACK TO:

41.   CRACK IN CEILING
It lengthens by half an inch.

42.   EXT. TUNNEL
as Curtin drives his burro up the trail. He is hauling water for the tank. He unloads the burro, pours the water into the tank, then starts back down the trail.

43.   INT. TUNNEL
Dobbs swinging his pick.

44. CRACK IN CEILING

It is twice as long now as before, and with each blow from the pick it gets wider.

45. CURTIN

starting his burro down the trail. He takes a few strides, hesitates, turns back up toward the tunnels. At the mouth of the first tunnel he calls to the old man.

CURTIN:
Hey, Howard, want me to spell you?

HOWARD:
Thanks, not right yet, baby. I'm just getting my second wind. (He turns around; with a movement of his arm he wipes the sweat and grime out of his eyes.)

Curtin moves on to the next tunnel. There has been a cave-in. The ceiling is hanging so low at the opening that there is not enough room for a body to pass through. Curtin doesn't take time to yell for Howard but starts clawing rubble aside. When he has made a big enough opening he wriggles into the tunnel.

46. INT. TUNNEL

Dobbs is lying unconscious, half covered with rock. Curtin works Dobbs's body free, then starts pulling him out. It is an inch-by-inch proposition getting the unconscious man through the narrow opening, but at last he succeeds.

CURTIN (shouting):
Howard! Howard!

Howard's VOICE answers hollowly from inside the tunnel.

HOWARD'S VOICE:
Yes?

The ring of Howard's pick against the stones stops.

CURTIN:
Come quick. Howard!

The old man comes on the run. One look at Dobbs's tunnel tells him what has happened. He immediately goes to work on Dobbs.

HOWARD (presently):
He's coming around.

Dobbs groans. His eyelids flicker, then open.

HOWARD:
Lie still for a minute till you get your senses back.

DOBBS:
What happened?

HOWARD:
Tunnel caved in on you.

DOBBS (remembers):
Yeah . . . I tell you I heard the harps playing sure enough. (He sits up now, tests his arms and legs.)

HOWARD:
Nothing broken.

DOBBS:
Guess I'm almost good as new. Who pulled me out?

HOWARD:
Curtin did.

There is a SOUND of falling rubble and the three men turn in time to see the tunnel sealed off for good. Dobbs shivers, then he stretches out his hand to Curtin.

DOBBS:
I owe you my life, partner.

CURTIN:

Forget it.

DISSOLVE TO:

47.   NIGHT

Howard is measuring out the yellow sand into three equal parts. Curtin and Dobbs follow his every move. Presently it is divided.

Dobbs takes up his share and leaves the circle of light the campfire makes to go off into the dark. The old man takes out his harmonica, begins to play softly.

CURTIN:

What are you going to do with your hard-earned money, old-timer, when you get back and cash in?

HOWARD:

I'm getting along in years. Oh, I can still hold up my end when it comes to a hard day's work, but I ain't the man I was once, and next year, next month, next week, by thunder, I won't be the man I am today. Reckon I'll find me some quiet place to settle down. Buy a business maybe . . . a grocery or a hardware store, and spend the better part of my time reading the comic strips and adventure stories. Once thing's for sure . . . I ain't going to go prospecting again and waste my time and money trying to find another gold mine . . . How's about yourself? What are your plans, if any?

CURTIN:

I figure on buying some land and growing fruit —peaches maybe.

HOWARD:

How'd you happen to settle on peaches?

CURTIN:

One summer when I was a kid I worked as a picker in a peach harvest in the San Joaquin Valley. It sure was something. Hundreds of people—old and young—whole families working together. After the day's work we used to build big bonfires and sit around 'em and sing to guitar music, till morning sometimes. You'd go to sleep, wake up and sing, and go to sleep again. Everybody had a wonderful time . . .

Dobbs comes back into the light of the campfire.

CURTIN (continuing):

. . . Ever since, I've had a hankering to be a fruit grower. Must be grand watching your own trees put on leaves, come into blossom and bear . . . watching the fruit get big and ripe on the bough, ready for picking . . .

DOBBS:

What's all that about?

HOWARD:

We've been telling each other what we aim to do when we get back.

DOBBS:

Me now, I got it all figured out what I'm going to do.

CURTIN:

Tell us, Dobbsie.

DOBBS:

First off I'm going to the Turkish bath and sweat and soak till I get all the grime out of my pores. Then I'm going to a barber shop and after I've had my hair cut and've been shaved and so on, I'm going to have 'em douse me out of every bottle on the shelf. Then I'm going to a haber-

dasher's and buy brand new duds . . . a dozen of
everything. And then I'm going to a swell cafe—
and if anything ain't just right, and maybe if it is,
I'm going to raise hell, bawl the waiter out, and
have him take it back . . . (He smiles, thoroughly
enjoying this imaginary scene at table.)

CURTIN:

What's next on the program?

DOBBS:

What would be . . . a dame!

CURTIN:

Only one?

DOBBS:

That'll all depend on how good she is. Maybe
one—maybe half a dozen.

CURTIN:

Dark or light?

DOBBS (the liberal):

I don't care what her nationality is just so long
she's kind of small and plump . . . you know
. . . (his hands describe an hourglass) . . . with
plenty of wiggle in 'er.[10]

HOWARD:

If I were you boys I wouldn't talk or even think
women. It ain't too good for your health.

DOBBS:

Guess you're right, seeing the prospect is so far
off.

HOWARD:

You know what. We ought to put some kind of
limit on our take. Agree between ourselves that
when we get exactly so much we pull up stakes
and beat it.

CURTIN:

What do you think the limit ought to be?

HOWARD:

Oh, say twenty-five thousand dollars worth apiece.

DOBBS:

Twenty-five thousand? That's small potatoes.

CURTIN:

How much do you say?

DOBBS:

Fifty thousand anyway. Seventy-five's more like it.

HOWARD:

That'd take another year at least . . . if the vein held out, which wouldn't be likely.

DOBBS:

What's a year more or less when that kind of dough's to be made?

HOWARD:

Twenty-five's plenty far as I'm concerned. More'n enough to last me out my lifetime.

DOBBS:

Sure, you're old. But I'm still young. I need dough and plenty of it.

CURTIN:

Twenty-five thousand in one piece is more'n I ever expected to get my hands on.

DOBBS (snorts):

Small potatoes!

CURTIN:

No use making hogs of ourselves.

DOBBS:
> Hog am I! Why, I'd be within my rights if I demanded half again what you get.

CURTIN:
> How come?

DOBBS:
> There's no denying, is there, I put up the lion's share of the cash?

CURTIN:
> So you did, Dobbsie—and I always meant to pay you back.

DOBBS (pointedly):
> In civilized places the biggest investor always gets the biggest return.

HOWARD:
> That's one thing in favor of the wilds.

DOBBS:
> Not that I intend to make any such demand, you understand, but I'd be within my rights if I did. Next time you go calling me a hog, remember what I could'a done if I'd'a wanted . . .

HOWARD:
> I think you're wise not to put things on a strictly money basis, partner. Curtin might take it into his head he was a capitalist instead of a guy with a shovel and just sit back and take things easy and let you and me do all the work.

While the old man talks, Curtin uses the scales to weigh out a portion of his dust.

HOWARD (continuing):
> He'd stand to realize a tidy sum on his investment without so much as turning his hand over. If anybody's to get more, I reckon it ought to be the one who does the most work.[11]

CURTIN (giving the dust to Dobbs):
> There you are, Dobbsie. What I owe you with interest.

DOBBS (he takes the dust, weighs it in his hand, then, with a sudden gesture, flings it away so that it falls, a little shower, into the fire):
> I just don't like being told I'm a hog, that's all.

HOWARD (addressing Dobbs):
> Other things aside, there's a lot of truth in what you were saying about being younger than me and needing more dough therefore. I'm willing to make it forty thousand apiece. (To Curtin.) What do you say, partner?

CURTIN:
> How long will it take?

HOWARD:
> Oh, another six months, I reckon.

CURTIN (after a moment's debate):
> Make it forty thousand or six months.

HOWARD:
> Suits me. Okay, Dobbs?

DOBBS (sourly):
> Okay.

HOWARD:
> Let's shake on it then.

The three men shake hands solemnly. Then Curtin gets up, starts away from the fire to hide his goods.

DISSOLVE TO:

48. INT. TENT CLOSE SHOT ON DOBBS   NIGHT
sleeping, a bar of moonlight across his face. OVER SCENE the SCREAM of a tiger. He stirs, turns over. The

SCREAM is repeated. Dobbs opens his eyes. Then he sits up, leaning on an elbow.

49. HOWARD'S BLANKETS

They're empty. CAMERA PULLS BACK TO FULL SHOT IN-TERIOR TENT. Curtin is in his blankets sound asleep. Dobbs frowns. After a moment Dobbs sits all the way up, throws back his blankets, reaches for his shoes, and puts them on. Then, picking up his revolver, he moves silently out of the tent and heads across the campsite. He's gone perhaps a dozen steps when he hears Howard coming. He draws back into the shadows. When Howard is scarcely three feet away, Dobbs steps out, suddenly confronting him.

DOBBS:
 That you, Howard?

HOWARD (startled):
 You oughtn't to go jumping out at me like that. I might've let you have it.

DOBBS:
 Out for a midnight stroll?

HOWARD:
 There's a tiger around. I went to see if the burros were all right.

DOBBS (grunts skeptically, then):
 So!

HOWARD:
 What's the matter, Dobbsie?

DOBBS:
 Think I'll make *sure* the burros are all right.

HOWARD:
 Help yourself.

He walks away in the direction of the tent.

50.   INT. TENT
as Howard enters. Curtin stirs.

CURTIN (to Howard, sleepily):
   What's up?

HOWARD:
   Nothing's up.

Curtin sees that Dobbs's blankets are empty.

CURTIN:
   Where's Dobbs?

HOWARD:
   Poking around in the dark out there.

51.   DOBBS
taking sacks of the precious dust out of his hiding
place—a hole underneath a rock. He is counting the
sacks aloud.

DOBBS:
   Three—four—five—six.

He gives a satisfied grunt, then starts putting them
back.

52.   INT. TENT
Howard has got back in his blankets.

CURTIN:
   He's sure taking a long time . . .

Curtin throws his blankets off, puts on his shoes.

CURTIN (continuing):
   I'm going to have a look-see.

53.   EXT. TENT
CAMERA PANS with Curtin to his hiding place—a hollow
tree. He begins to pick out his sacks of gold.

54.   INT. TENT
as Dobbs enters. He starts to take his shoes off, then notices Curtin's absence.

DOBBS (sharply):
     Where's Curtin?

HOWARD:
     Out there some place. He said something about having a look-see.

Again Dobbs's brow becomes furrowed with suspicion. He puts his shoe back on, gets up, and is about to leave the tent when Curtin enters. He and Dobbs survey each other wordlessly.

HOWARD:
     It's come around to me again, but I won't take my turn if you guys'll quit worrying about your goods and go to bed. We got work to do tomorrow.

Dobbs grunts, turns back into the tent. Curtin drops down on his blankets.

                                            DISSOLVE TO:

55.   EXT. THE MINE   CLOSE SHOT   DOBBS
at the sluice, washing sand and talking to himself.

DOBBS:
     You can't catch me sleeping . . . Don't you ever believe that. I'm not so dumb. The day you try to put anything over on me will be a costly one for both of you.

At the OVER SCENE SOUND of hoofs on rock, Dobbs stops talking. CAMERA PULLS BACK to show Curtin driving two of the burros. Dobbs keeps his face averted and Curtin passes without any words being exchanged. As the SOUND of the hoofs fades, Dobbs resumes his monologue.

DOBBS:

> Any more lip out of you and I'll pull off and let you have it. If you know what's good for you, you won't monkey around with Fred C. Dobbs.

56.   CURTIN

at a turn of the trail. He comes upon the old man repairing a tool.

CURTIN:

> You ought to get a load of Dobbsie. He's talking away to himself a mile a minute.

HOWARD (shaking his head):

> Something's eating him. I don't know what. He's spoiling for trouble.

Curtin grunts, proceeds on down the trail.

57.   DOBBS

DOBBS (mimicking Howard's voice):

> We're low on provisions, Dobbsie. How about you going to the village. (Then as Dobbs again.) Who does Howard think he is, ordering me around?

HOWARD'S VOICE (OVER SCENE):

> What's that, Dobbsie?

Dobbs looks up in surprise. CAMERA PULLS BACK to a CLOSE SHOT of Howard and Dobbs.

DOBBS:

> Nothing.

HOWARD:

> Better look out. It's a bad sign when a guy starts talking to himself.

DOBBS (angrily):

> Who else have I got to talk to? Certainly not you or Curtin. Fine partners, I must say.

HOWARD:

Got something up your nose?

Dobbs doesn't answer.

HOWARD:

Blow it out. It'll do you good.

DOBBS (shouts suddenly):

Don't get the idea you two are putting anything over on me.

HOWARD:

Take it easy, Dobbsie.

DOBBS (still louder):

I know what your game is.

HOWARD:

Then you know more than I do.

DOBBS (railing):

Why am I elected to go to the village for provisions—why me instead of you or Curtin? Don't think I don't see through that. I know you've thrown together against me. The two days I'd be gone would give you plenty of time to discover where my dust is, wouldn't it?

HOWARD:

If you have any fears along those lines, why don't you take your dust along with you?

DOBBS:

And run the risk of having it taken from me by bandits.

HOWARD:

If you were to run into bandits, you'd be out of luck anyway. They'd kill you for the shoes on your feet.

DOBBS:

So that's it. Everything is clear now. You're hoping bandits'll get me. That would save you a lot of trouble, wouldn't it? And your consciences wouldn't bother you either!

HOWARD:

Okay, Dobbs, you just forget about going. Curtin or I'll go.

Dobbs turns on his heel, stalks off.

58.   PAN SHOT OF CURTIN
Something he sees out of scene causes him to stop.

59.   A GILA MONSTER
Curtin picks up a rock, but before he can heave it the big yellow and black lizard has disappeared under a boulder. Curtin drops the rock, picks up a piece of timber, runs one end underneath the rock making a lever. He leans his weight on the end of the timber.

DOBBS'S VOICE (OVER SCENE):
Just like I thought.

Curtin turns. CAMERA PULLS BACK to show Dobbs covering Curtin with his gun.

CURTIN:
What's the idea?

DOBBS:
Put your hands up.

Curtin obeys. Dobbs takes Curtin's gun away from him.

DOBBS:
I got a good mind to pull off and pump you up, chest and belly alike.

CURTIN:

Go ahead and pull, but would you mind telling me first what it's all about?

DOBBS:

It won't get you anywhere playin' dumb.

CURTIN (comprehension dawning on his face):

Well, I'll be—so that's where your dust is hidden, Dobbsie?

Howard comes up.

HOWARD:

What's all the hollerin' for?

CURTIN:

Seems like I stumbled accidentally on Dobbs's treasure.

DOBBS (snorts):

Accidentally! What were you trying to pry up that rock for? Tell me that!

CURTIN:

I saw a gila monster crawl under it.

DOBBS:

Brother, I got to hand it to you. You can sure think up a good story when you need one.

CURTIN:

Okay. I'm a liar. There isn't any gila monster under there. Let's see you stick your hand in and get your goods out. Go ahead.

DOBBS:

Sure I will. But don't you make a move or I'll . . .

CURTIN:

Don't worry. I'll stand right where I am. I want to see this.

Dobbs goes down on one knee beside the boulder. He starts to put his hand in, hesitates, then bends forward to look into the hole.

CURTIN:

> Reach right in and get your goods. If you don't we'll think you're plain yellow, won't we, Howard?

Dobbs sneaks his hand forward toward the opening beneath the rock.

CURTIN:

> They never let go, do they, Howard, once they grab onto you—gila monsters. You can cut 'em in half at the neck and their heads'll still hang on till sundown, I hear, but by that time the victim don't usually care anymore because he's dead. Isn't that right, Howard?

HOWARD:

> I reckon.

CURTIN:

> What's the matter, Dobbs, why don't you reach your hand right in and get your treasure? It couldn't be you're scared to, could it, after the way you shot off your mouth. Show us you aren't yellow, Dobbsie. I'd hate to think my partner had a yellow streak up his back.

DOBBS (sweat showing on his face—the sweat of fear; he springs to his feet, aims wildly at Curtin, shouting):

> I'll kill you, you dirty, thieving . . .

But before he can pull the trigger Howard has knocked up his arm. Then both men close in on him. Curtin gets the gun away from him.

CURTIN:

> Okay, Howard, I got him covered. Dobbs, an-

other bad move out of you, and I'll blow you to kingdom come. Hey, Howard, turn that rock over, will you.

Howard obeys, leaning his weight on one end of the timber until the rock rolls over. CAMERA MOVES INTO A CLOSE-UP of a gila monster, its body arched, hissing, atop Dobbs's treasure. OVER SCENE the SOUND of a shot. The slug bores through the lizard's head, its body rises, its tail threshes.

60.   CLOSE-UP   DOBBS
his face is white, his eyes are staring.

CUT BACK TO:

61.   CLOSE-UP   THE GILA MONSTER
lying belly up on Dobbs's treasure, his arms clawing at the air.

SLOW DISSOLVE:

62.   A TYPICAL DURANGO VILLAGE
A scattering of adobe huts, a church, a cantina, and a general store. Entering the village behind his two burros, Curtin sees that something is going on in the square. The townspeople make a circle around a half dozen Federales whose Lieutenant is talking to two mestizos, tough-looking fellows in big hats and blankets such as the bandits that attacked the train were. From the edge of the crowd, Curtin sees the Lieutenant open a billfold and take out money and a small rectangle of cardboard. He holds up the cardboard for everybody to see. All the talk is in Spanish so Curtin doesn't know for sure what's happening.

LIEUTENANT (opening billfold):
No hay ninguna duda, ustedes son, después del asalto al tren les seguimos la pista. Miren, que más pruebas, la cartera con el boleto. La misma fecha. Ya verán lo que les va a pasar por bandidos.

Curtin ties his burros to the hitching post outside the general store, then addresses the Storekeeper who stands in his doorway watching the proceedings in the square.

CURTIN:
> Buenos días, amigo.

STOREKEEPER:
> ¿Cómo está usted, señor?

CURTIN:
> What is going on?

STOREKEEPER:
> Son de los bandidos que han estado asaltando trenes. Mire, el Teniente le encontró a ese una cartera robada con un boleto de ferrocarril.

Curtin shakes his head, unable to understand.

STOREKEEPER (continuing):
> Ese par ya tiene días aquí tomando tequila como agua, escandalizando y sembrando el miedo por todas partes.

OVER SCENE another VOICE speaks. Curtin turns in surprise for the words are English with an American accent.

CODY'S VOICE:
> The Lieutenant just found a railroad ticket in a woman's purse the big fellow had on him. The ticket has on it the date of the Agua Caliente train robbery.

> CAMERA PULLS BACK TO:

63.   MED. SHOT CODY
in foreground. He is about thirty-five, tall, but not husky. His manner, well bred but decisive.

CODY (continuing):
Between them they had a diamond ring, two pearl earrings, and quite a lot of money. It seems they've been here in this village several days drinking and shooting off their cannons so that the villagers are afraid to stick their noses out of their huts.

The Lieutenant now addresses a small boy upon whom the honor of holding the Lieutenant's horse has been bestowed. The boy points. The Lieutenant motions with his head for the two bandits to move along in the direction the boy pointed. Then he mounts and follows. The Federales and townspeople bring up the rear.

CURTIN:
What'll they do with them now? Where are they taking them?

CODY:
To the cemetery.

CURTIN:
Oh. (He enters the store.)

64. INT. STORE
The Storekeeper goes around behind his counter.

CODY (who has followed Curtin in):
The Federales are very efficient in their way. It may not be our American way. They aren't fingerprint experts, that is, but they can follow any trail, and against them no hideout's any use. They know all the tricks of the bandits. You can bet your sweet soul that they'll run down every last one of those groups that attacked the train. It'll take time— months—maybe—but they'll do it.[12]

Curtin doesn't want to prolong the conversation, which may lead to questions he doesn't wish to answer. At the same time he doesn't want to awaken, by his reticence, the other man's curiosity. He "hmmmmms" politely, turns to the Storekeeper, and begins to point out various articles on the shelves—salt, coffee, cornmeal, soap, etc.

CODY:

> Not many Americans get around this way. You're the first I've bumped into for a long time.

CURTIN:

> That so.

CODY:

> Mighty rough country hereabouts.

CURTIN:

> Yep.

CODY:

> My name's Cody. I'm from Texas. (He puts out his hand.)

CURTIN (shakes hand):

> Curtin.

CODY:

> What's your game?

CURTIN:

> I'm a hunter.

CODY:

> Professional?

CURTIN:

> Yep.

CODY:

> What all do you hunt?

CURTIN:

> Oh, tiger cats—anything with a hide of commercial value.

CODY:

I should think you'd do better west of here—on the Rio Conchos, for example. Lot better hunting ground over that way.

CURTIN:

I'm doing all right.

CODY:

How long'd you say you'd been in these mountains?

CURTIN:

Few months.

CODY:

Seen anything that looks like pay dirt?

Curtin shakes his head no.

CODY (continuing):

I've got an idea there's truckloads of the real goods up in those mountains.

CURTIN:

Well, I know the whole landscape around, and if there was a single grain of gold you can bet I'd sure seen it. No, there's nothing doing here for gold.

CODY:

Listen, brother, I can look at a hill five miles away and tell you whether it carries an ounce or a ship-load. If you haven't found anything up there yet I'll come along with you and put your nose in it. There's indications in this valley, lots of indications, and by tracing the rocks I found that they come from that ridge up there, washed down by the tropical rains.

CURTIN:

You don't say so.

CODY:

Yes, I say so.

OVER SCENE the SOUND of a volley.

CODY:

So much for those bandits. You got to hand it to the Mexicans when it comes to swift justice. Once the Federales get their mitts on a criminal they know what to do. They put shovels in their hands and tell 'em to dig and when they've dug deep enough they tell 'em to put their shovels down and have a cigarette and say their prayers. And in another five minutes they're being covered over with the earth they dug out.

Through the open doorway the Federales, led by their Lieutenant, can be seen departing on horseback.

CURTIN:

Yep, you got to hand it to 'em all right.

The Storekeeper counts on his fingers, then tells Curtin the amount owed. Curtin pays him, carries the sacks and tins out of the store.

65.   EXT. STORE

as Curtin goes about loading up the burros. Cody comes out of the store.

CODY:

I meant what I said about going along with you. Those are my two mules. I'm all packed up and ready to start if you'll let me come with you back to your camp . . .

CURTIN:

Thanks just the same, but I prefer going it by myself. (He tightens the hitches on the burros, unties the lead rope, and starts off. Without looking back he calls.) Good luck.

66.   PAN SHOT   CURTIN
as he passes the cemetery. The townsmen are throw-
ing dirt into the graves.

DISSOLVE TO:

67.   LONG SHOT   DESERT PLAIN
that leads up to the mountains. Far in the distance six
moving specks, three widely separated from three.

DISSOLVE TO:

68.   CLOSE SHOT   CURTIN AND HIS BURROS
Curtin turns around, frowns. Below him and some
distance behind, another man with pack animals is following in his tracks. Curtin proceeds another dozen
yards, then stops. The frown becomes a scowl.

69.   LONG SHOT
The first three dots are not moving. The second three
remain in motion for a time. Then they also stop.
After a brief period the first three start again, then
sure enough, the second three also start.

DISSOLVE TO:

70.   MED. SHOT   CURTIN
as he turns into a rocky defile. He advances some
dozen yards, then pulls his burros into a draw, ties
them to a sapling, and turns back to the entrance of
the defile. He takes a position behind a rock. Presently the SOUND of hoofs can be heard, then Cody's
figure, beating his two mules, comes INTO SCENE. Curtin takes out his revolver, twirls the chamber to see
that it's working smoothly, then waits for Cody to
come abreast. When that occurs he steps out from behind the rock.

CURTIN:

What's the idea you following me? Don't make
me sore, you mug, or you may get hurt. I don't
go butting into your business, and you better not
into mine. Believe me, mug, I could take care of

116

you any day of the week if you were twice your size. So if you know what's healthy for you, you better lay off and quit following me.

CODY:

I didn't mean to bother you. I only want to be in the company of an American for a change and sit for a few nights by a fire and smoke and talk.

CURTIN:

Well, I don't want to talk, see. And I've heard all the talking out of you I want to, so turn around and start the other way.

Seeing he means business, Cody obeys. Curtin goes back to his burros, waits until the footfalls of Cody's mules can no longer be heard, then unties his own burros and starts on.[13]

DISSOLVE TO:

71.   THE CAMPSITE   HOWARD, DOBBS, AND CURTIN   NIGHT
around the campfire. Supper is cooking.

CURTIN:

. . . I went way around and kept on hard ground which wouldn't show tracks. I even drove the burros through long stretches of brush to get the mug off my trail. But whenever I reached a high point and looked back I could see he was coming right along. I guess it's only a matter of time until he shows up here.

DOBBS:

I move we tell him straight off to beat it. And if he don't then we fill his belly up with plums too hard for him to digest.

HOWARD:

That'd be foolish. He'd sit around for an hour playing the innocent and then go and report us to the officials. Once they were here we couldn't stay any longer. And we couldn't take our goods with us when we left.

DOBBS:

All right. Then there's nothing else to do but pull the trigger the minute he appears.

Howard stirs a pot that is on the fire.

HOWARD:

It's no crime to visit these mountains. He may be a guy that just likes to roam around. We can't shoot him for that, and besides if we were to shoot him it might come out.

DOBBS:

We don't have to shoot him necessarily. We could push him off a rock and claim it was an accident.

HOWARD:

And just who's going to do the pushing? You, Dobbsie?

DOBBS:

We could play odd man . . .

HOWARD:

Brother, count me out!

DOBBS:

You're sure he was trailing you, are you?

CURTIN:

Absolutely.

DOBBS:

How come?

Curtin makes a gesture with one hand and glances toward an opening in the bushes where the path leads.

CURTIN:

Because there he is.

Howard and Dobbs are so bewildered that for a few seconds they cannot bring themselves to look around.

DOBBS:
Where?

Curtin nods toward the path. Howard and Dobbs finally turn around and there in the deep shadows of the falling night, uncertainly lighted by the flickering campfire, stands the stranger between his two mules.

CODY (finally after a long silence):
Hello.

Presently Dobbs rises. With long, slow strides he crosses to the stranger. Then, hands in his pants pockets, he looks him up and down.

DOBBS:
Come over to the fire.

CODY:
Thank you, friend.

He comes close to the fire, starts taking the packs off his mules. None of the others offers to help him. Dobbs drops down by the fire. Howard takes the pot of potatoes from the fire, shakes it, and tests the potatoes with a knife to see whether they are cooked enough. Curtin gets up and brings more wood, then puts on the coffee can. Dobbs simply lies sprawled out watching every move Cody makes. The silence becomes interminable.

CODY (suddenly):
I know quite well, you fellows, that I'm not wanted around here. (No one denies this; he addresses himself to Curtin.) But even after what you told me on the trail I simply couldn't resist the desire to sit around and jaw with an American.

DOBBS:
Then why don't you go where there are Americans that might want to talk to you? Durango isn't

so far off. All the American clubs you could hope for are there.

CODY:

I'm not after that. I've got other things on my mind—more important.

DOBBS:

So've we. And don't you make any mistake. Our biggest worry right now is your presence here. We've no use for you. We don't even want you for a cook or a dishwasher. We're full up. No vacancy. Understand? If I haven't made myself clear, let me tell you I think you'll be doing yourself a big favor if you saddle up first thing in the morning and go where you came from and take our blessing with you.

The newcomer remains silent. He watches the three partners deal the meat and potatoes out on the plates and fall to eating.

CURTIN (over his half-emptied plate):

Help yourself, partner, to a plate and spoon and knife and fork.

DOBBS:

Sure. We're no misers. We don't let guys starve to death. Help yourself. Tonight you're welcome. But beginning tomorrow look out. No trespassing around here. You know—dogs! Get me?

Dobbs gives Curtin a long wink, then:

DOBBS (continuing):

I got five foxes and a lion while you were away to the village.

CURTIN:

Good hides?

DOBBS:

Pretty good.

CODY (without emphasis):
> Excuse me for butting in, but there's no game here worth going after. It wouldn't take one week for a real hunter to clean up all around for five miles in each direction.

Dobbs is on his feet instantly, his right hand hovering around the butt of the revolver that is stuck inside his waistband.

HOWARD (sharply):
> You're right. There's no good hunting here. That's why we've made up our minds to leave this ground inside a week and look for something better. Yep, stranger, you're dead right. This here's awful poor ground. It took us some time to find it out.

CODY:
> Poor ground, you say? Depends on what you're hunting for. For game, yes. But it's very good ground for something else.

HOWARD:
> And what might that be?

CODY:
> Gold.

Dobbs's hand closes around his revolver butt. Howard shoots him a fierce look.

HOWARD:
> Gold, did you say. Ha-ha—that's a good one.

CURTIN:
> I told you at the village, mister—there's no gold hereabouts.

HOWARD (laughs):
> My boy, if there were one single ounce, I'd have seen it. Believe me I would.

CODY:

> If you haven't found any gold here then good night, sir. You aren't as smart as you appear to be.

This last serves to confound the partners. Howard clears his throat, then he nods.

HOWARD:

> Maybe . . . maybe you're right. Who knows. We never had a thought about gold. Gives me an idea. I'll sleep over it. (He stretches.) Guess I'll hit the hay.

CURTIN:

> Me too. (He gets up.) Until tomorrow, mister.

Cody doesn't answer.

CURTIN:

> G'night.

Cody whistles. In a few moments his two pack mules come hobbling up. He gives each a handful of corn which he takes from his pack, then after patting their necks, he kicks them lightly and they return to the shadows. Going a little way off from the fire, Cody spreads his blankets and lies down to sleep. Only then does Dobbs leave the campfire and enter the tent.

72.   INT. TENT

The other two are already stretched out.

DOBBS:

> I can't figure that bird out. Is he wise to us or ain't he?

HOWARD:

> Whether he is or not, he looks fairly harmless to me.

DOBBS:

Looks can be mighty deceiving.

HOWARD:

There's no denying that.

DOBBS:

I'm of the opinion we ought to get rid of him—the quick way. How about me starting a quarrel with him? Make him boil over and then as soon as he draws, all of us blast away at him.

CURTIN:

That don't sound too pretty, the way you put it.

DOBBS:

For all we know he might have it in his head to murder us all in our sleep this very night.

HOWARD:

Anything's possible.

DOBBS (excitedly):

Well then?

HOWARD:

Tell you what. You guys go to sleep. I'll be watchdog for a couple of hours. Then you and Curtin can have your turns.

DOBBS:

Okay. Is your gun handy?

HOWARD:

Yep. (His hands are tranquilly folded across his chest.)

Dobbs crawls into his blankets. OVER SCENE the VOICE of the coyotes yip-yipping.

73.   CLOSE-UP DOBBS
as he goes to sleep, begins to snore.

74.   CLOSE-UP HOWARD
This is all he's been waiting for; hearing Dobbs snore,
he closes his eyes and falls asleep.

DISSOLVE TO:

75.   EARLY MORNING
The braying of a jackass awakens Dobbs. He looks at
Curtin and Howard, sees they are both asleep, then
plunges out of the tent. The stranger is by the fire,
making coffee.

CODY:
Good morning, friend.

DOBBS (ignoring the greeting):
Where'd you get the water to make coffee?

CODY:
I just took it from the bucket.

DOBBS:
Oh you did, did you. Well, that water wasn't carried up here so's you could make coffee, see.

CODY:
I'm sorry. I didn't know water was so hard to get.

DOBBS:
Well you know it now.

CODY:
I'll go fill the bucket up for you.

Curtin, followed by Howard, comes out of the tent,
observes Dobbs's belligerent attitude.

CURTIN:
What's up?

DOBBS:
This mug has been stealing our water. (To Cody.)
Let me catch you at it once again and I'll let it out
of you in little round holes.

CODY:

I thought that perhaps I was among civilized men who wouldn't begrudge me a little fresh water.

DOBBS:

Who ain't civilized?

Without waiting for an answer he plants his fist in the stranger's face with such force that Cody drops full length as if felled by a heavy club. Then Dobbs busies himself at the fire as do Curtin and Howard. It takes Cody some time to come to. When he does, he rises and shakes his head to discover whether his neck is broken. Then he comes close to Dobbs.

CODY:

I could easily do the same to you, and it isn't settled yet who'd come out on top. This time I took it. Thanks for your kind attention.

The stranger's words and his manner of speaking embarrass Dobbs and make him feel ashamed. He shifts awkwardly.

HOWARD:

If I was you, mister, I'd saddle up and go while the going's good.

CODY:

But I mean to stay right here.

DOBBS AND CURTIN (together):

How's that?

CODY:

The brush and the mountains are free, aren't they?

HOWARD:

That's right, friend, to whoever is first on the spot.

CODY:

> That holds for hunters, but not for gold miners. Unless, of course, they've registered their claim. I take it you guys haven't registered yours.

CURTIN:

> Who said we had a claim to register?

CODY:

> Whatever you say or don't say, tomorrow I start to dig for gold here.

Unseen and unheard, another presence joins the now silent group—murder is amongst them. Solid and real as if made of flesh and bone. All their thoughts are upon this new companion in their midst. The problem of what to do about Cody is insignificant compared to the decision each of the partners must now make—to kill or not to kill. Cody, fully realizing that his life hangs by the most delicate thread, takes a deep breath, begins to talk.

CODY:

> Oh, I know quite well you can bump me off any minute you wish, but that's a risk worth running, considering the stakes. Let's lay all our cards on the table. As I see it, you fellows have got to do one of three things: kill me, run me off, or take me in with you as a partner. Let's consider the first. Another guy might show up tomorrow, or maybe a dozen guys. If you start bumping people off, how far are you prepared to go with it? Ask yourselves that. Also, don't forget that the one actually to do the bumping off would forever be in the power of the other two . . . the only safe way would be for all three of you to pull your cannons and bang away at the same instant like a firing squad. (He indicates Dobbs.) He'd be all for that I'm sure, but you two haven't the look for born executioners.

HOWARD:

We wouldn't stop at anything in protecting our interests.

CODY:

I claim killing me isn't it. But of course, that's for you to decide. As for choice number two, if you chase me off I might very well inform on you.

HOWARD:

We'd get you if you did that. We'd go all the way to China to get you. There'd be no quarter.

CODY:

Nevertheless, you'd still come off losers.

Howard nods, then:

HOWARD:

Wouldn't the knowledge that we'd follow you till doomsday make you think twice before informing on us?

CODY:

I'd think twice all right. But that doesn't say I wouldn't turn you in. Twenty-five percent of the value of your find is the reward I'd get paid and that would be mighty tempting—mighty tempting.

CURTIN:

That's a pretty strong argument in favor of our doing number one, mister.

CODY:

I don't deny it, but let's see what number three has to offer. If you take me in as a partner you don't stand to lose anything. I will not ask to share in what you've made so far . . . only in the profits to come. Well, what do you say?

The three partners sit silently for several moments. Then:

HOWARD:

>Would you mind, stranger, letting us three thrash this out alone among ourselves?

CODY:

>Not at all. Go ahead. I have to look after my mules anyway.

CAMERA PANS Cody away.

76.　CLOSE SHOT OF THE THREE
watching him go.

DOBBS (when the stranger is out of earshot):

>Where does he get off pushing his way in here after all the work we've done. Soft pickings for him, ain't it. Whoever else happens along—are they to be invited in too? Is it a come-one-come-all proposition?

HOWARD:

>Sending him away is out of the question, all right. Either we bump him off or make him a partner.

DOBBS:

>Do the mug in I'd say. He himself told us the way. All three of us let him have it so there won't be any question of its being held over anybody's head in time to come.

77.　MED. SHOT CODY
moving across a high rock. Something OUT OF SCENE makes him slow his pace and finally stop.

78.　LONG SHOT ONTO THE PLAIN BELOW THE MOUNTAIN
A dozen or so dots are moving toward the mountain and the CAMERA. The dots are men on horseback.

79.　CLOSE-UP CODY
watching intently.

80.   CAMP   DOBBS, HOWARD, CURTIN

HOWARD:

What's your feelings in the matter, Curtin?

CURTIN:

I'm all for protecting our interests, but what do we gain by bumping him off? Nothing, so far as I can see. If he was asking to share in what we've made so far it'd be a different story.

DOBBS:

Fred C. Dobbs ain't a guy who likes being taken advantage of.

HOWARD:

I don't mind being taken some advantage of so long as it ain't money out of my pocket. What the devil . . . we can throw all the dirty jobs at him.

CODY'S VOICE (OVER SCENE):

Come up here! Come quick!

The partners look around in surprise.

CODY'S VOICE:

Come on. Hurry!

The three start running in the direction of the rock. But before they've gone about a dozen yards, Dobbs stops suddenly.

DOBBS:

Wait. Maybe he's up to something—a trick—like rolling a rock down on us or something. You go that way, Howard; and you, Curtin, that way. If he's pulling a trick we'll all let him have it.[14]

Dobbs takes his revolver out, starts up toward the rock, moving slowly.

81.   CODY   ON THE ROCK

He calls again.

CODY:

    Hurry up.

Howard is first to appear on top of the rock.

CODY (pointing):

    Look!

Howard squints his eyes.

HOWARD:

    I can't make out what they are.

Curtin is next, followed after an interval by Dobbs.

HOWARD (continuing):

    Must be soldiers.

Dobbs turns on Cody, draws his gun, and cocks the hammer with his thumb.

DOBBS:

    So that's your stinking game, is it? All right—take what's coming to you. (He points the gun to Cody's chest.) I knew you were an informer. I knew it all the time. If you know a prayer, you rat, say it now and make it snappy.

CODY (in a quiet voice):

    You're wrong, partner. This means all our funerals, my own included.

CURTIN:

    What's that?

CODY:

    If I'm right in what I'm thinking then may the Lord be with us. They're not soldiers. Bandits—that's what they are. And they aren't after gold but guns and ammunition . . . The villagers must have told them about the American hunter up here.

CURTIN:

    They don't look like soldiers to me either, but just what he says—a bunch of dirty, ragged bandits.

HOWARD:

> We're in a hole, I tell you. With soldiers we'd at least have a chance to explain before an official. But with bandits . . .

DOBBS:

> I still think you're an informer . . .

CURTIN:

> Shut up, Dobbs. Leave him alone. We've got to think and work fast now.

DOBBS (on his single track):

> . . . not an informer for the government—an informer for the bandits.

CODY:

> Wrong again, brother. And if you don't lay off me you may find yourself short one full-grown man. Inside an hour or so you're going to need not only every man here but every hand and every gun.

HOWARD:

> We better start thinking about a way to defend ourselves. We might try hiding in the rocks but then we'd lose the burros and our whole outfit so I guess the best thing is to make a fight of it. (He points at a ravine, narrow and not very deep, that lies between the rock on which they stand and the camp.) That ravine is a good natural trench. If we make our stand there, they can't attack from the rear and they can't flank us. They'll have to pass over the campsite and we'd get some good shots at them. Cody, you seem to have good eyes—you stay up here on this lookout for the time being and watch their movements. You, Curtin, round up the burros and herd them into that thicket over there. Dobbs, let's you and me wrap up all our belongings and dump 'em into the trench.

They hasten to the task of preparing for the assault that is to come.

82. DOBBS
filling buckets with water and carrying them to the trench.

83. CURTIN
getting the burros.

84. CODY
on the rock, watching the approach of the bandits.

85. HOWARD
piling rocks in front of the trench.

CODY (OVER SCENE):
They're turning onto the trail up here.

HOWARD (calls):
How many of them are there?

86. CODY
watching the approach of the bandits.

87. LONG SHOT BANDITS
riding the trail that leads to the camp.

88. CLOSE-UP CODY
as he calls:

CODY:
Sixteen of 'em.

89. CLOSE SHOT HOWARD
He calls to Cody.

HOWARD:
Come on down, friend. I guess we're about as ready for 'em as we ever will be, so we might as

well have something to eat. They'll be the best part of an hour getting here.

He starts laying a fire. The partners, Cody included, gather around.

CODY:
One of 'em's wearing a hat painted gold. It reflects the sunlight . . .

CURTIN:
A hat painted gold. Hear that, Dobbs, Howard! Remember the bandit in the gold hat?

DOBBS:
Sure, on the train!

HOWARD:
Him—huh!

DISSOLVE TO:

90.   THE FOUR MEN IN THE TRENCH
They have just finished eating.

HOWARD:
If nobody objects, I'll take command. Right by you, partners?

CURTIN:
Right.

CODY:
No objection.

DOBBS:
Sure.

HOWARD:
I'll take the left center. You, Cody, take the right. Dobbs, your station is the left corner, and Curtin, you take the right corner. The left corner is the most important. A guy could sneak through that crack in the rocks over there.

They go to their various posts. Presently there comes the SOUND of hoofs. Finally the bandits appear, one after the other, coming up the trail. They carry guns of different types and caliber. All are in rags and are unwashed and unshaven. A few have boots, half ripped open and with torn soles. Some wear leather pants like rancheros. They dismount. Two of the bandits venture forward into the campsite. They observe where the tent has been pitched and they point to the remnants of the fire. They call to the others who come forward and begin walking around the place, peering behind bushes and rocks. A discussion commences in the middle of the camp. There seems to be very little discipline. Each man has his own opinion and talks louder than the next.[15]

AD LIBS:

> FIRST MAN: Hace poco acamparon aquí. SECOND MAN: Miren muchachos, vengan aquí. THIRD MAN: No vámonos, aquí nos embotellan. FOURTH MAN: Los que estaban aquí ya se fueron este es un magnífico escondite.

HOWARD (to Curtin in a whisper):

> They think whoever was here is gone. Some of them want to go back down the mountain and some want to stay up here and use this site as a headquarters from which to raid villages in the valley.

CURTIN:

> How about pouring it into them and bumping off as many as we can right away fast.

HOWARD:

> Hold your horses.

Two of the men begin to build a fire. One exploring for wood leaves the others and comes straight across the camp toward Dobbs's station. He is looking upward at a growth of saplings so that he is hardly five feet away from Dobbs before he sees him. For a moment his jaw hangs in surprise, then he turns around and shouts:

BANDIT:

Miren muchachos, vengan todos. Pronto ... Una pajaríta echada en su nido. Qué cosa más bonita.[16]

The others all rise and come hurrying toward him. When they are halfway across the camp, Dobbs shouts.

DOBBS:

Stop or I shoot.

FIRST BANDIT:

Ya, Ya, está bien. Espere. No tire, hombre.[17]

He walks backward, making no attempt to reach for the heavy revolver at his side. The bandits hold a rapid-fire consultation, speaking in lowered tones so that the men in the trench cannot make out a word. Then Gold Hat steps forward, thumbs close together in front of his belt to indicate that he does not mean to go for his weapon.

GOLD HAT:

Oiga, señor. Listen, we are no bandits. You are mistaken. We are Federales; you know, the mounted police. We are looking for the bandits to catch them. The ones who robbed the train you know.

DOBBS:

All right. If you're the police, where are your badges?

GOLD HAT:

Badges? We got no badges. We don't need badges. I don't have to show you any stinking badges.

Again he starts forward. Four or five of the others move to follow their leader. Dobbs yells.

DOBBS:

> You better not come any closer if you want to keep your health.

GOLD HAT:

> No sea malo, hombre. We don't want to do you any harm. No harm at all. Why can't you be a little more polite? We mean well. Give us your gun and we'll leave you in peace. Sure we will.

DOBBS:

> I need my gun myself.

GOLD HAT:

> Throw that old iron over here and we'll pick it up and go on our way.

DOBBS:

> Nothing doing. You better go without my gun— and go quick before I lose my temper.

Dobbs waves his gun over the rim of the trench. The bandits retreat a few steps and then hold council again.

HOWARD:

> They'll be playing some kind of a trick now.

Sure enough. Gold Hat, the leader, and another stand up, move toward Dobbs. The second bandit has a gold watch dangling by a chain in his outstretched hand. He is slightly in advance of Gold Hat.

GOLD HAT:

> Look here, amigo, you got the wrong idea. I don't want to have your gun for nothing. I want to buy it. Here I have a genuine gold watch with genuine gold chain made in your own country. That watch and chain is worth at least two hundred pesos. I'll

exchange it for your gun. Good business it is for you. You better take it.

The other bandit swings the watch on its chain around his head.

DOBBS:
You keep your watch. I'll keep my gun.

GOLD HAT:
Oh you will? You'll keep it, eh? We won't get it? I'll show you, you . . .

There is a SHOT. The bandit with the watch throws up both hands so that the watch and the revolver fly through the air.

BANDIT (in Spanish):
Estoy herido. I am hit.

Grabbing at his side he falls and begins crawling back to the others.[18]

91.   HOWARD
He is looking through his peephole over the sights of his rifle. It was he who fired the shot.

92.   BANDITS
All of the bandits, including Gold Hat, look in the direction from which the shot came. It wasn't Dobbs who had fired. At the opposite corner of the trench a faint cloud of blue smoke still hangs in the air. The bandits all move backward toward the bushes.

93.   MED. LONG SHOT   BANDITS
They are squatting on their heels, having another discussion. Suddenly Gold Hat gets up, laughing.

GOLD HAT (he calls to Dobbs):
Hey, señor. You there. You cannot play such tricks on us. We know that you had your rifle

over there . . . and that by means of a long string you pulled the trigger from where you are. We do the same when hunting ducks at the lakes. Don't try this on us.

With a rapid move all the men have their guns up.

GOLD HAT (continuing):
And now come out of your dirty hole. No stalling any longer. Come. Vámonos or we'll drag you out like a rabbit. And when we get you out we will tear open your mouth to your ears.

The men drop to the ground and, guns in hand, start crawling toward the trench. Hardly have they advanced six feet when there are four SHOTS from the trench, each from a different gun. All the bandits turn around without getting up and crawl back into the bushes. There are shouts in Spanish back and forth between them. The bodies of two of the bandits remain where they fell in the area between the trench and the campsite.

HOWARD (to Curtin):
That'll keep 'em for a while. We've won a breathing space I figure. (He leaves his position and goes to Cody.) Good work, Cody.

CODY:
Do you think we've beat them off for good?

HOWARD:
Hardly. Now that they know that there's at least four guns here, they'll be more determined than before.

CODY:
What do you suppose they'll pull next?

HOWARD:
They'll probably attack just before morning.

He leaves Cody and moves back past his own station to Dobbs.

DOBBS:

> We got 'em on the run now. How about us attacking?

HOWARD:

> Nope. It's better not to give away our number. For all they know there's a dozen of us. We're pretty safe here in this trench. If we prayed to the Lord things couldn't be better. The moon, for instance. It'll be full. The campsite will be flooded with moonlight so's even a cat can't cross without our seeing. We'd better change our stations for the night and stay in two groups. Cody and I'll take the right section and you and Curtin the left so's one can nap and the other watch. As soon as things start to happen, you just kick the sleeping guy in the ribs and he'll be up. I'm positive there won't be any move on the other side for the next six hours. It'll be different around four in the morning. Why don't you take your sweet slumber now?

DISSOLVE TO:

94. NIGHT

as Cody shakes Howard awake.

CODY (in a hushed voice):
> I think they're coming.

Howard moves quickly to Dobbs's and Curtin's post. They are both awake.

HOWARD:

> Hold your fire till four men reach the middle of the camp. Then shoot to kill.

He goes back to his post.

95.   MED. LONG SHOT ON CAMP

as the bandits move over the ground. FOUR SHOTS ring out. There are groans and cries of Holy Mother. The bandits keep on coming. One of the bandits springs upright and charges the trench. He has a revolver in one hand, a machete in the other. He reaches the trench where Cody is before he falls. None of the others ever gets so close to the trench. Their reception is too hot. The night attack is a failure. Once again they crawl back on their bellies toward the bushes.

HOWARD:

   Looks like we won that round.

Cody, at his post, doesn't answer.

HOWARD:

   Hey, Cody.[19]

He turns to him. Cody is dead, a bullet through his neck.

DISSOLVE TO:

96.   ALL MEN AT THEIR POSTS

including Cody, toward whose body the others look somberly now and again. OVER SCENE the SOUND of wood being chopped.

DOBBS:

   I wonder what dirty business they're hatching right now.

HOWARD:

   I got a pretty good idea.

DOBBS:

   What?

HOWARD:

   They're making barricades that move. It's an old Indian trick. They crawl along pushing the barricades before them. You can't see where to shoot. Brother, I'd be willing to trade our gold mine right now for three or four hand grenades. If that's what they're up to, and I'm dead sure it is, we haven't a Chinaman's chance.

DOBBS:

All we can do is sell our lives at the highest price possible. I mean to take as many of 'em as I can to hell with me.

HOWARD:

Don't forget to save one last bullet for yourself. God forbid any of us fall alive into the hands of those we wounded. If you can't shoot yourself, try to stab yourself to death.

CURTIN:

Maybe if we offer them our goods and our guns they will let us off.

DOBBS:

Not a chance, baby boy. They'd torture us just the same to find out if there isn't more than we offered them. Then they'd kill us just the same. They don't know what mercy is.

HOWARD:

Know why? Because they've never been shown any. If our people in the States had lived in poverty under all sorts of tyrannies for hundreds of years they'd have bred a race of bandits too, every bit as cruel and bloodthirsty. Come right down to it we are bandits of a kind. What right have we got to go looting their mountain anyway? About as much right as the foreign companies that take their oil without paying for it . . . and their silver and their copper.[20]

OVER SCENE beyond the campsite an excited voice calls:

VOICE:

Compadre, compadre. Muy pronto.

DOBBS:

What's up I wonder.

OVER SCENE the voices of the bandits mingle in rising excitement. The SOUND of the chopping leaves off.

CURTIN:

Something's happening all right.

OVER SCENE THE SOUND of the bandits saddling their horses and mounting. Curtin starts to climb out of the trench.

DOBBS:

Wait, pal, this may only be a trick to lure us out and get us.

HOWARD:

I don't think so. They aren't good enough actors for this to be a trick.

Curtin, not heeding Dobbs's warning, leaves the trench and climbs up to the high place where Cody first saw the bandits.

97.   LONG SHOT   WHAT CURTIN SEES

In the far distance a marching squadron of cavalry.

CURTIN (calls):

Hey, partners, up here. Here's a sight if there ever was one.

Dobbs and Howard climb rapidly up to Curtin.

DOBBS:

Soldiers, look at 'em. I could kiss every one of them.

CURTIN:

They must have got it from the villagers that bandits had gone up this mountain to rob the gringo hunter of his guns and provisions.

DOBBS:

> I can't get it why the bandits are leaving. Why don't they wait for the soldiers up here?

HOWARD:

> Because they're old fighters who know all the tricks, that's why. With us at their backs and the soldiers facing them they wouldn't have a chance. Their only hope is to get out of this canyon before the soldiers enter.

DOBBS:

> Anyway they're doing us a big favor by leaving in such a devilish hurry. It wouldn't have been too healthy for us to have soldiers up here. They could be a real nuisance to us fellas if they started asking questions and nosing around.

98.   LONG SHOT   THE BANDITS

riding hard. They reach the mouth of the canyon, turn to the right. They are caught sight of by the column of cavalry which goes into a gallop.

DOBBS:

> Go get 'em! Sic 'em Tige! Chew 'em into bits and don't spit 'em out—swallow 'em . . . Am I happy, am I. Fellers, tell you the truth I was already chewing dirt.

CURTIN:

> Too bad they didn't arrive before what's-his-name got his.

HOWARD:

> Reckon we couldn't have held out the night without his assistance. I'd say providence had sent him to us except . . .

DOBBS:

> Except what?

HOWARD:
>   Why should providence put a smaller value on his life than on one of ours?[21]

CURTIN:
>   I wonder who he is and if he's got any folks?

DOBBS:
>   Supposin' he has.

CURTIN:
>   We ought to notify them.

HOWARD:
>   Let's take a look at his belongings.

Howard shakes himself out of his thoughts. The three start back down from the high place.

99.   CLOSE SHOT   OF THE DEAD CODY
lying face down in the same defensive position he held when alive. Howard's hands COME INTO SCENE and turn him over. They feel in Cody's pockets, bring out a wallet and some letters.

100.   CLOSE SHOT   OF THE THREE
as Howard opens the wallet.

HOWARD (examining the contents):
>   Couple hundred dollars. Name's James Cody. This here driver's license was issued in Dallas, Texas. Letter's from Dallas too, so that must be his home. (He takes a snapshot out of the wallet.) Real pretty, ain't she. His girl, I reckon.

DOBBS:
>   Let me see.

101.   SNAPSHOT IN DOBBS'S HAND
Young woman with a tender, smiling face.[22]

102. SCENE
There is something about the way Dobbs is looking at the picture that Curtin doesn't like.

DOBBS:
Not bad, not bad.

Curtin reaches out and takes the snapshot from Dobbs's hand. Howard has removed the letter from the envelope and is scanning it.

HOWARD (reading):
Dear Jim: Your letter just arrived. It was such a relief to get word after so many months of silence. I realize, of course, that there aren't any mail boxes that you can drop a letter in out there in the wilds, but that doesn't keep me from worrying about you. Little Jimmy is fine, but he misses his daddy almost as much as I do. He keeps asking, "When's Daddy coming home?" You say if you do not make a real find this time you'll never go again. I cannot begin to tell you how my heart rejoices at those words if you really mean them. Now I feel free to tell you. I've never thought any material treasure, no matter how great, is worth the pain of these long separations.

The country is especially lovely this year. It's been a perfect spring—warm rains, hardly any frost. The fruit trees are all in bloom. The upper orchard looks aflame and the lower like after a snow storm. Everybody looks forward to big crops. I do hope you are back for the harvest.

Of course, I'm hoping that you will at last strike it rich. It is high time for luck to start smiling upon you, but just in case she doesn't remember we've already found life's real treasure. Forever yours, Helen.[23]

He holds out the letter for the others to read.

103.   INSERT POSTSCRIPT
A child's scrawl, big letters and little letters and things that are like letters but aren't. Then a hieroglyphic "Jimmy."[24]

104.   SCENE
Curtin gives him back the snapshot. Howard puts it into the wallet, and he puts the wallet and the letter back into his pocket. Then he picks up a spade from the pile of equipment at the bottom of the trench. He climbs out of the trench, stands looking around for a moment, selecting a proper site, then he starts digging a grave.

                                        FADE OUT

FADE IN
105.   CAMPFIRE   NIGHT
The old man is measuring out the gold into three parts as we have seen him do before.

HOWARD:
Only seven penny-weight thirteen grains.

DOBBS:
Less than we did yesterday.

HOWARD:
If you want my opinion it's going to keep getting less from now on. We've taken about all the gold this here mountain has.

DOBBS:
How much do you figure we've made to date?

HOWARD (wets the end of his lead pencil, figures on a piece of paper):
Not as much as we were aiming to collect—not forty thousand—not that much.

CURTIN:
I'm willing to lower my hindsights.

HOWARD:

> We got upwards of thirty-five thousand apiece—
> and we ought to be plenty thankful.

DOBBS:

> Sure—let's call it quits and pack up and leave.

HOWARD:

> It's going to be a lot harder trip going back than it
> was coming. The burros' loads are heavier and
> accidents will be more likely to happen on the
> trail. There's always the danger of bandits, of
> course, but added to that there's another hazard
> that wasn't there before—the Federales. If we
> were to meet up with them they might get kind
> of curious about what we're carrying in our
> packs. Oh, we got the goods all right, but I don't
> figure it's really ours until we pass it over the
> counter at the bank.

CURTIN:

> We been mighty lucky so far. Here's hoping our
> luck holds.

DOBBS:

> Yeah, here's hoping. Sooner we leave the better,
> as far as I'm concerned. I don't want to keep that
> dame waiting, whoever she is.

HOWARD:

> It'll take us another week to break down the mine
> and put the mountain back in shape.

DOBBS:

> Do what to the mountain?

HOWARD:

> Make 'er appear like she did before we came.

DOBBS (mystified):

> I don't get it.

HOWARD:

> We've wounded this mountain and it's our duty to close her wounds. It's the least we can do out of gratitude for all the wealth she's given us. If you guys won't help me I'll do it alone.

CURTIN (laughs):

> You talk about the mountain like it was a real person . . .[25]

DISSOLVE TO:

106.   FULL SHOT   EXT. MINE

or rather what was once the mine. Howard's wishes have been carried out and the place looks almost the same as before the three men came to take the mountain's gold. The water system—wheel, vats, and sluices—is afire. The burros stand patiently while the three men load them up.

HOWARD:

> Well, I reckon that's about everything. Go get your goods, boys, and I'll get mine and we'll be off.

Each man goes to the hiding place of his gold, gets it out and, staggering under its weight, brings it back to where the burros are. They go about loading on the sacks and covering them with hides.

HOWARD:

> I reckon each man's burro with his goods better be his own responsibility.

The others nod.

DOBBS:

> Let's get going.

They start, Curtin in the lead, across the campsite area. Coming to the spot where Cody is buried, Curtin slows down but doesn't stop. When they reach the opening in the brush where the trail begins, Howard turns and looks back.

HOWARD (waves):
Good-by, mountain, and thanks.

DOBBS (imitates Howard's gesture):
Yeah, thanks, mountain.

CURTIN (waving at the mountain):
Thanks.

DISSOLVE TO:

107.   LONG SHOT   DESERT
It is not the flat mesquite-littered kind of desert but an arid rocky wasteland full of gullies and ledges with an occasional giant cactus standing sentinel. The heat waves rising from the ground distort the air so that the whole tortured landscape swims constantly before the eyes of the three men. They move at a slow pace, timing their steps to those of the heavily loaded burros. Something frightens the lead burro who shies suddenly and begins to back. Howard looks OUT OF SCENE.

108.   A RATTLESNAKE
coiled a few yards ahead. Howard leads his burro off to the right, giving the snake a wide enough berth. He makes no move to destroy the snake nor do the others who simply follow in Howard's steps.

DOBBS (calls to the snake over his shoulder):
This is your domain. No argument, brother. We're trespassing. We don't like being here any more than you like having us. You just tell us a shorter way out and we'll take it.[26]

DISSOLVE TO:

109.   EXT. THE WILDS   TWILIGHT
The three partners are around a campfire preparing their evening meal. The hobbled burros are grazing

nearby. The bags of gold are in three separate stacks. The food is on the fire, and Dobbs and Curtin are stretched out doing nothing beyond listening to Howard's harmonica. There is something lonely and haunting about its music.

CURTIN:

I been thinking about her—Cody's widow, I mean—and the kid. You know what . . . ? We'd oughta give 'em a fourth just as if he'd been partners with us from the start.

DOBBS (his jaw drops, then):

You mean a fourth of all our goods?

CURTIN:

Yeah, that's right.

DOBBS:

Are you crazy?

CURTIN:

If it hadn't been for Cody we wouldn't've walked away from that mountain. Ask Howard.

HOWARD:

Yep, the buzzards would've got fat on us all right.

DOBBS:

It might just as well've been one of us. That it wasn't is our good luck and his bad.

CURTIN:

Whatever you guys do I'm going to give a fourth.

HOWARD:

What the devil—I got more than I need anyhow. Half what I got is enough to last me out. A fourth—sure.

DOBBS:

You guys must've both been born at revival meetings.

Howard has lowered his harmonica. Now, head cocked in an attitude of listening, he sits staring into the surrounding bush.

HOWARD:
Pipe down.

DOBBS (after a brief silence, whispers):
What's up?

Howard takes out his revolver, twirls the chamber, then moves away from the fire into the shadows. He motions to the others and they do likewise. Then all at once four Indians appear. They are unarmed and of innocent appearance. One of them addresses the partners in Spanish.

FIRST INDIAN:
Buenas noches, señores. ¿Podemos sentarnos cerca de la lumbre? Descansar un poquito. ¿Por favor?

HOWARD (to the Indians):
Con mucho gusto, cómo no, amigos. ¿Quieren tomar café con nosotros?

INDIAN:
Sí, muchas gracias, señores.[27]

HOWARD (to Dobbs and Curtin):
Whatever they want they mean no harm.

He gestures and Curtin offers them a cup. The Indians help themselves, all drinking out of the same cup. Dobbs produces his tobacco pouch. This they also accept, each taking a pinch of tobacco and rolling it in corn leaves which they carry on them. In return they offer the partners tobacco of their own.

DOBBS:
We give them tobacco and they give us tobacco. I don't get it. Why not everybody smoke his own?

HOWARD:

Take some and thank them.

Dobbs and Curtin obey, saying "Muchas gracias."

HOWARD:

They're after something. It'll take them awhile to come to the point. To say what you want right off the bat isn't considered polite among Indians.

A long silence ensues, during which the Indians drink their coffee and smoke their cigarettes. Each time they raise the cup they smile at the white men. Finally, the speaker among them begins:

INDIAN:

Pués verá usted señor. Mi hijito se cayó al agua y lo sacamos tan pronto como pudimos. No se mueve, ni nada y no se quiere revivir, pero yo creo que no está muerto. Necesitamos ayuda, por favor.

HOWARD:

¿Cuándo sucedió esto a su hijito?

INDIAN:

Este tarde, señor.

HOWARD (to the partners):

His little boy fell into the water. They fished him out but he won't come to. He isn't dead. He just won't come to.

Howard gets to his feet.

HOWARD:

I'll go and have a look at the boy and get back here as soon as I can, before morning probably. Watch after my goods while I'm gone. (He turns again to the Indians.) Bueno, amigos, yo voy con ustedes. No sé si podré ayudar, pero haré todo lo posible. Vámonos.

The Indians all get up, politely take leave of Dobbs and Curtin. They lead Howard to the horse, which he mounts, then leading the way they run off on foot.

110.   INT. ADOBE HUT

A palm mat is spread over a table upon which a small boy lies motionless. The room is crowded with Indians, both men and women. Howard enters behind the boy's father. The Indians stand aside making a pathway to the table. Howard goes to the boy, stands over him silently for a time, trying to decide what the treatment should be. With his thumb he raises the child's eyelids, then, ear to chest, he listens for a heartbeat. He tries artificial respiration. This treatment makes a deep impression on the Indians who look at each other and murmur approvingly.

HOWARD:

> Quiero agua caliente. Unas toallas. También un espejo y un poco tequila. (To four Indians.) Ustedes froten mucho manos y pies, pronto.[28]

While these things are being produced, Howard instructs four of the Indians on how to rub the boy's hands and feet so that the blood is sent toward the heart. When the hot towels are ready, he places them on the boy's belly, after which he forces open the boy's mouth and pours into it a teaspoonful of tequila. Presently he listens again for the heartbeat. His eyes light up. There is life in the little body.

HOWARD:
Dame el espejo.

He holds it to the boy's mouth. Sure enough it shows a faint mist. A murmur runs through the room. Howard goes on with the artificial respiration. After a little while the boy coughs. The murmur is repeated. It is hardly a murmur—it is rather that slight sound that accompanies a quick intaking of breath. The onlookers believe they are seeing a miracle performed. Shouting or any other sign of jubilation would be unseemly. They act as if they were under a spell. And now the boy opens his eyes. No single word is uttered by anyone present. They simply look at the awakened boy and at Howard in awe.

Howard helps the little boy to sit up. The child looks around him, wonderingly, at all the faces, his eyes finally resting on the strange bearded face of the white man. Then his mouth puckers up and he begins to cry. Except for the crying of the child, there is no other sound in the room, not even the shuffling of feet. Howard puts his hand briefly on the little boy's head, then turns to go.

HOWARD:
Buenas noches.

No answer is made. Again the way is cleared for him. The eyes of the Indians turn with him as he passes, and they are full of awe.

DISSOLVE TO:

111.   EXT. MOUNTAINS   DAY
FULL SHOT   OF THE PARTNERS AND THEIR BURROS
moving along the trail.

HOWARD:
Artificial respiration did it and some Boy Scout tricks. I think it was more shock than drowning. He hadn't swallowed much water. Maybe he was stunned when diving.

OVER SCENE from a distance, the SOUND of a voice—a man's voice in a long drawn-out call.

DOBBS:
Now what!

CURTIN:
We've got something on our heels.

Looking in the direction of the call, they see a number of horsemen come INTO VIEW. Again they reach for their weapons and make ready to defend themselves, but when their pursuers arrive they are the Indians of the night before. The partners put their weapons aside and greet them. As before, it is the father of the little boy who does the talking.

INDIAN:

¿Porqué se van tan pronto, señores?

HOWARD:

Tenemos negócios importantes en Durango.

INDIAN:

Pero señores, no se vayan tan pronto. Queremos que estén con nosotros aunque sea unas semanas.

HOWARD:

Muchas gracias por la invitación. Pero necesitamos estar en Durango en una semana.[29]

INDIAN:

Pero señor, usted salvó la vida a mi hijito. Si lo dejo que se vaya sin mostrarle gratitud no tendré perdon de Dios.

DOBBS (to Howard):

What's up?

HOWARD:

He's insisting that we return with him to his village and be his guests. He wants to pay off his debt to me for saving his son's life, by feasting and honoring us. Otherwise he believes he'll burn in Hades.

DOBBS (laughing):

Tell him to forget it. He don't owe you a thing.

HOWARD (to the Indian):

Mi mayor recompensa fue el gusto que sentí cuando el nino abrió los ojos.

INDIAN:

Pero señor, tengo que pagarle mi deuda. Si no se me enojarian todos los Santos del Cielo. Venga por favor.[30]

HOWARD (to his partners who are laughing at him):

This is no laughing matter. I'm afraid he's determined to show his gratitude even if it means taking us back to the village as prisoners.

DOBBS (cutting in):

Sabe, hombre. No podemos quedar. *No.* No. Imposible, ¿sabe?

Dobbs pushes through the Indians, roughly. They let him pass, but form a determined circle around Howard.

INDIAN (to Dobbs):

Usted o él no importa. (Pointing at Curtin [*sic*]): Este señor sí importa.

CURTIN:

What did he say?

HOWARD (anxiety showing plainly on his face):

It makes no great difference what you two do, but I have to come.

DOBBS:

So it's like that. They only want you.

HOWARD:

Looks like it.

DOBBS:

Okay. Go with 'em. Stay a few days, then follow us to Durango. We'll meet you there.

HOWARD:

What about my packs?

CURTIN:

Take them along with you.

DOBBS:

I'm against that. If they were to discover what's in them they might forget you were their honored guest and rob you or even kill you. In any case, word would get out and then no trail would be safe for you to travel alone.

HOWARD (at a loss):

All right. What'll I do—spill my goods out right here on the ground?

CURTIN:

We'll take 'em with us if you want us to and wait for you in Durango. If you're held up longer than a week or so we might go on to the port and deposit your goods at a bank there.

HOWARD (after a pause):

I reckon that's about the only solution there is.

Curtin takes out a piece of paper and a pencil.

CURTIN:

If we don't meet at Durango your goods'll be deposited in the Banking Company. We'll tell the manager you hold this receipt. We'll leave our signatures with him to identify you. Here's a receipt. Okay?

HOWARD:

Okay. Maybe after I've stayed with 'em a little while these fellows will let me have a horse to ride to Durango. I may get there only a day or two behind you.

Curtin gives him the receipt.

CURTIN:

That'll be fine. Good luck, old man.

First Curtin, then Dobbs shake hands with Howard.

DOBBS:

> Yeah, all the luck in the world. We'll sure feel lonesome without you, but like my Sunday school teacher said, "We have to swallow disappointments in this sad life."

CURTIN:

> Hurry up and join us.

DOBBS:

> Don't go getting mixed up with any of those Indian dames. Pretty smart some of 'em are. Look out a squaw don't marry you.

He slaps Howard's back.

HOWARD (trying to joke):

> Maybe I'll do just that. Pick me out a good-looking squaw and marry her. They're easy to feed and dress and entertain. And they don't nag at you either. So long, partners.

He turns away so that they don't see the mist in his eyes. The Indian indicates which horse Howard is to ride. After the old man has mounted, the Indian gets up behind him in the saddle. Shouting joyfully, they start back toward the village.

DOBBS AND CURTIN (together):

> See you in Durango.

Dobbs and Curtin turn to the burros and start the train once more on its way.

DISSOLVE TO:

112.   EXT. THE VILLAGE

as the troop of Indians enter with Howard. It's an occasion for great celebration. Young and old people are awaiting him. They cheer him as though he had returned from some victory in foreign lands for the greater glory of their village. Howard's dismounting is the cue for the fiesta to begin. He is the center of ev-

erything. It is to him the musicians play and the singers sing; for him the dancers dance.[31]

DISSOLVE TO:

113.   EXT. MOUNTAINS   A HIGH, STEEP PASS
Dobbs and Curtin, their breath coming in agonizing
gasps, struggle up the trail, beating the burros, pushing them on, shoulder to quarters. Every few yards
they have to halt to give their pounding hearts a rest.

DOBBS (raises the water bottle to drink):
> Isn't it always his burros that won't march in line
> and stray off and smash their packs against the
> trees and rocks. I wish they'd break off the trail
> and drop down a few thousand feet of gorge and
> crash their bones. What was in your head when
> you offered to carry his goods? As if he couldn't
> manage by himself. He knew what he was doing
> when he turned them over to us. Mighty cute of
> him, wasn't it?

CURTIN:
> What's the use of railing against the old man. It
> won't do any good. Save your breath for that next
> piece of trail.

DOBBS:
> I'm stopping here for the night. If you want to go
> on it's okay by me, only take the old man's bur-
> ros with you. They ain't my responsibility.

CURTIN (looking at the sun):
> It's still early. We might make four or five miles
> more before dark.

DOBBS:
> No one's ordered you to camp here. You can go
> twenty miles more for all I care.

CURTIN (losing his temper):
> Ordered me? You? Who's ordering who to do

159

anything? You talk like you were boss of this outfit.

DOBBS:

Maybe you are. Let's hear you say it. (He looks as
though he were ready to spring upon Curtin.)

CURTIN:

Okay, if this is as far as you can go.

DOBBS:

Who says it is? (He advances a step on Curtin; his
face is dark and wicked looking in his anger.)
Don't make me laugh. I can go four times as far
as a mug like you. I don't want to go any further
that's all. I could but I don't want to. See, mug!

CURTIN:

What's the good of hollering. We're started on
something. Like it or not, we got to finish it. All
right, let's camp here.

DOBBS:

That was my idea in the first place.

He begins to unload the burro standing next to him.
Curtin comes close and gives him a hand at the job.

DISSOLVE TO:

114.   DOBBS AND CURTIN BY THE CAMPFIRE   NIGHT

CURTIN:

I wonder what the old man's doing now?

DOBBS:

Finishing a meal of roast turkey and a bottle of
tequila most probably.

CURTIN:

This is the first day we've had to handle everything without his help. Once we get the hang of
it, it'll be lots easier.

DOBBS:

How far from the railroad do you think we are?

CURTIN:

Not so far as the crow flies.

DOBBS:

But we ain't crows.

CURTIN:

I figure we can make the high pass in two days more. Then it'll be three or four days before we get to the railroad. That's figuring no hard luck on the trail.

Curtin puts more wood on the fire. Dobbs sits staring into space. All at once he laughs.

CURTIN (looks around at Dobbs):
What's the joke?

Dobbs laughs again, louder this time.

CURTIN:

Won't you let me in on it, Dobbsie?

DOBBS:

In on it? Sure I will. Sure. (He keeps on laughing.)

CURTIN:

Well, go ahead. Spill it. What's so funny?

DOBBS:

It just came to me what a bonehead play that old jackass made when he put his packs in our keeping.

CURTIN:

How do you mean?

DOBBS:

Figured to let us do his sweating for him, did he? We'll show him! (He laughs again.)

CURTIN:

What are you getting at?

DOBBS:

Man, can't you see? It's all ours now. We don't go back to the port, savvy? Not at all.

CURTIN (unable to believe his ears):

I don't follow you, Dobbsie.

DOBBS:

Don't be such a sap. Where'd you grow up? All right, to make it plain to a dumb-head like you—we take all the goods and go straight up north leaving the old jackass flat.

CURTIN:

You aren't serious are you? You don't really mean what you're saying?

DOBBS:

I never say anything I don't mean.

Curtin puts another stick of wood on the fire, then he gazes up at the clear night sky.

CURTIN (finally):

As long as I can stand on my two legs you won't take a single grain from the old man's goods. You understand?

DOBBS (craftily):

Sure, babe. Sure I do. I see very plainly what you mean. You want to take it all for yourself and cut me out.

CURTIN:

No, Dobbs. I'm on the level with the old man. Exactly as I'd be on the level with you if you weren't here.

DOBBS (takes up his pouch and starts filling his pipe):

Maybe I don't need you at all. I can take it alone. I don't need no outside help, buddy. (He laughs.)

CURTIN (looks him over from head to foot):
I signed that receipt.

DOBBS:
So did I. What of it? I've signed many receipts in my life.

CURTIN:
I guess I've signed things, too, which I forgot about before the ink was dry, but this case is different. The old man worked like a slave for what he got. It was harder on him old as he is than it was on us. I don't respect many things in life, but one thing I do respect—a man's right to what he's worked and slaved for honestly.

DOBBS:
Get off your soapbox, will you. You only succeed in sounding funny out here in the wilderness . . . Anyway, I know you for what you are. I've always had my suspicions about you. Now I know I've been right.

CURTIN:
What suspicions are you talking about?

DOBBS:
You can't hide anything from me, brother. I see right through you. For some time you've had it in your mind to bump me off at the first good opportunity and bury me somewhere out here in the bush like a dog so's you could make off not only with the old man's goods but with mine in the bargain.[32]

Curtin shakes his head in a dazed way. His pipe drops from his fingers.

DOBBS (continuing):
When you reach the port safely you'll laugh like the devil, won't you, to think how dumb the old

man and I were not to guess what was brewing.
I'm wise to you, babe.

Curtin looks into Dobbs's eyes, at once fascinated and
terrified by the malignancy he sees. He tries to pull
his eyes away from Dobbs—cannot. To cover his agi-
tation he bends down to pick up his pipe. Dobbs, mis-
taking this for hostile, draws his gun.

DOBBS:
Another move, brother, and I pull the trigger. Get
your hands up. (Shouting.) Up, up!

Curtin raises his hands.

DOBBS:
Higher.

Curtin obeys. Dobbs smiles, satisfied, nods his head.

DOBBS:
Was I right or was I? You and your Sunday
school talk protecting other people's goods. You.
(Yells suddenly.) Stand up and take it like a man.

Curtin rises slowly, his hands still in the air. Dobbs
reaches for Curtin's gun. As he does so his own gun
goes off. For a fraction of a second he is surprised.
Curtin, instinctively sensing his opportunity, lands
Dobbs a hard blow on the jaw, knocking him to the
ground. He throws himself upon Dobbs quickly and
disarms him. Then he springs up and steps a few
paces back.

CURTIN (two guns pointed at Dobbs):
The cards are dealt the other way now, Dobbsie.

DOBBS:
So I see.

CURTIN (calmly):
Listen to me. You're all wrong. Not for a moment
did I ever intend to rob you or do you any harm.

Like I said, I'd fight for you and yours just as I'd
fight for the old man.

DOBBS:

If you really mean what you say then hand over
my cannon.

Curtin waves the gun in his hand, then breaks it open
and empties the cartridges out. He throws it up in the
air, catches it cowboy fashion, then holds it out toward Dobbs. Dobbs looks at it sneeringly.

DOBBS:

My pal.

He spits, then retires to his former place by the fire. A
long silence follows, broken only by Curtin.

CURTIN:

Wouldn't it be better, the way things stand, to
separate tomorrow—or this very night?

DOBBS:

That would suit you fine, wouldn't it.

CURTIN (perplexed):

Why me more than you?

DOBBS:

So you could fall on me from behind, sneak up,
and shoot me in the back.

CURTIN:

I'll go ahead.

DOBBS:

And wait for me on the trail and ambush me? My
pal.

CURTIN:

Why shouldn't I do it here and now if I meant to
kill you?

DOBBS:

> I'll tell you why. You're yellow. You don't dare
> pull the trigger while I'm looking at you in the
> eye that's why.

CURTIN (shakes his head again):

> If you think that, I can't see any way out but to
> tie you up every night.

DOBBS (sneering):

> Come on and try to tie me up.

Curtin and Dobbs sit looking at each other. Both men
are exhausted after the hardships of the day. Curtin
knows he is in for a night of horror. He cannot afford
to go to sleep even if Dobbs does, for how is he to
know if Dobbs is really asleep? Or, on the other hand,
if Dobbs is not feigning, what is to keep him from
waking up? Curtin yawns.

DOBBS (laughs):

> I'll make you a bet. Three times thirty-five is a
> hundred and five. I bet you a hundred and five
> thousand dollars you go to sleep before I do.

He laughs again.

DISSOLVE TO:

115.   EXT. THE TRAIL   DAY

The pack train on the move, Dobbs in the lead. Curtin
walks like a man in a trance, stumbling every so often
out of exhaustion brought on by the sleepless night.

Now his eyes are actually closed. He is holding on
to one of the burro's packs, letting the animal guide
his steps. Observing this, Dobbs halts and stands
aside on the trail, letting the train pass. Some instinct
causes Curtin to open his eyes just before coming
abreast of Dobbs.

CURTIN (reaching for his gun):

> Get up there ahead of the train.

Grinning, Dobbs obeys.

DISSOLVE TO:

116.   CAMPFIRE   OFF THE TRAIL   NIGHT

As on the night before, the two men sit a few feet
apart, facing each other. Curtin's eyes finally begin to
blink. He gets up, walks back and forth. Dobbs never
stops looking at him. Presently Curtin sits down
again. It is not long before his head drops forward.
Dobbs starts to crawl over to him. Curtin jerks awake
and draws his gun. Dobbs laughs.

DOBBS:

A born night watchman. I have to hand it to you.
You should try for a job at a bank.

Dobbs stretches out full length, lies on his side, looking at Curtin. Curtin's eyes start blinking again. Each
time he opens them it is a greater effort. It is as
though heavy weights are attached to each lid. Finally
they remain closed. Not that Curtin is asleep—it is
simply that his eyes need a few seconds' rest. He is
determined not to go to sleep—determined. Both fists
are clenched with the effort. Even after his head has
dropped forward on his chest the knuckles show
white.

When Curtin's breathing is deep and regular, Dobbs
gets up, goes over to him, and relieves him of his
gun. Then he kicks Curtin hard in the ribs.

DOBBS:

The cards are dealt once more—another way, and
this is the last time. No more shuffling.

CURTIN (tries to rise; mumbles):

What cards do you mean?

DOBBS:

Stay where you are. I'm going to finish things up
right now. No more orders from you such as I
had to swallow today. Get me?

CURTIN (he is too sleepy to comprehend all that is going on about him; voice thick):
> You mean you're going to murder me?

Dobbs kicks him again to arouse him.

DOBBS:
> No, brother, not murder. Your mistake. I'm doing it to save my life which you'd be taking the first instant I stopped looking at you.

CURTIN:
> Don't forget the old man. He'll catch up with you. Just wait and see.

DOBBS:
> Yeah? Will he? Well, I got the answer for that when the time comes. You want to know what I'll tell him? I'll tell him you tied me to a tree and made your getaway with all the goods—yours, mine, and his. Then he'll be looking for you, not for me.

He laughs as if this were the best joke he'd ever heard. Curtin, fighting to keep awake, tries to shake the sleepiness out of his system, but fails. Dobbs kicks him again.

DOBBS:
> Up now, and march where I tell you. Today I had to march to your music—now you're to march to mine.

CURTIN (lurches upright):
> Where to . . . march?

DOBBS:
> To your funeral.

Curtin moves in a dream. Dobbs grabs him brutally by the collar, pushes him ahead into the brush.

DOBBS:
> Keep going.

CURTIN:

Please, let me have just another hour's sleep. I'm all in. I can't march any longer. And let the burros have another hour too. The poor beasts—they're all overworked and their backs are sore. (He falls.)

DOBBS (kicks Curtin):

Get up. Keep going. You'll have time enough to sleep in a minute.

Curtin staggers again, with Dobbs close behind, pushing and kicking. When they are far enough in the bush to suit Dobbs, he draws his pistol and shoots.

Curtin goes down like a felled tree. Dobbs stands over him for a few seconds, pistol in hand. Then he bends down and listens briefly. Hearing no sigh and no moan, he rises and, putting his pistol back in the holster, returns to the campfire where he sits and stares into the flames. Presently he turns his face around toward the bush where Curtin is. It's as though he expected Curtin to appear out of the darkness.

DOBBS (to himself):

Maybe I didn't bump him off. Maybe he only staggered and dropped to the ground without being hit.

His eyes turn back to the fire where they remain staring. Suddenly he jumps up, takes a thick piece of burning wood out of the fire to use as a torch, and rushes back into the bush.

Curtin is lying motionless in the same spot where Dobbs had left him. Dobbs leans over, goes to put his hand against the breast of his victim, then jerks his hand away. He holds the burning stick near Curtin's face, moving it back and forth, but there is not even the flicker of an eyelash.

Dobbs straightens up and turns away again, but before he goes ten feet he pulls out his gun, squares around, and lets Curtin have another shot to make absolutely sure. Having fired the gun, he looks at it.

DOBBS (to himself):

> It'll look better this way. (He throws the gun to-ward where Curtin lies, mutters.) It's his anyhow. (Then he goes back to the fire and resumes his former position; he shivers.) This fire don't give any real heat. I'd ought to've brought more sticks in before dark. I won't go back into the bush now and get them. (He gets his blanket and rolls up in it.) They won't find him. I'll dig a hole first thing in the morning.

He closes his eyes. Suddenly they are open and he is sitting up, staring into the surrounding bush; then he laughs to himself.

DOBBS:

> Conscience. Conscience. What a thing. If you be-lieve you've got a conscience, it'll pester you to death. But if you don't believe you've got one, what can it do to you? Makes me sick so much talking and fussing about nonsense. (Assuming a matter-of-fact tone.) Time to go to sleep.

He closes his eyes, but not for long. After a few seconds they're open again and he is staring into the fire.

DISSOLVE TO:

117.   MORNING

Dobbs is just finishing the loading of the burros which is not easy without the help of a second man. His shirt is drenched with sweat and his impatience amounts to rage. He kicks one of the beasts savagely when a pack slips, as though it were the burro's fault. By the time the pack train is ready to start, the sun is high in the heavens. But there is one more task await-ing Dobbs. He has left a spade on the ground in an-ticipation of it. He picks up the spade and starts into the bush, but he only goes a step or two before stopping.

DOBBS:

> Might be better to leave him where he is. Ain't very likely anybody would happen on him in there. If they did they'd just as like to find a grave as a body. Bandits wouldn't have buried him. In a week's time the tigers and wild pigs and the buzzards and the ants will have done away with him entirely.

While he is standing thus, irresolutely arguing with himself, there is a CRY from not far distant, shrill as a woman's scream. It cuts into Dobbs like a knife. His hands start trembling and he totters in his tracks.

DOBBS:

> What's getting into me? That was only a tiger.

He pulls himself together and, in an attempt to shake off his fear, takes another step forward into the bush. Again he falters.

DOBBS:

> No. What if his eyes were open. I don't dare look at his eyes. Best thing is to hurry and try and reach the railroad soon as possible.

He leaves the bush, goes back to the burros, shouts at them. The train is once more on its way. But immediately trouble begins. A burro goes out of his way to scrape against a rock. The pack shifts on his back so that its weight is all on one side of the animal, who staggers, then falls. Dobbs must unhitch the burro, get him back on his feet, and do the whole job of packing him up over again. While he is about this, the other animals scatter. At last he succeeds in rounding them up and getting them all onto the trail again. But his difficulties have only started. When he marches at the head of the train, the animals in the rear stray off and when he is at its rear, the leader either stops or goes off the trail. He has to run up and down the train like a dog keeping a flock of sheep together. But presently, through Dobbs's strenuous efforts, the animals are all in single file and going in the right direction.

DOBBS (resuming the argument with himself):
> Better not to bury him. I did right. Yeah. The chance of anybody happening on him inside a week is a mighty slim one . . . and there won't be much of anything left of him by then. Only his clothes . . . What I should've done maybe . . . undressed him and buried his clothes and left him for the wild pigs and the ants and the buzzards . . .

He stops suddenly. An appalled expression comes over his face.

DOBBS:
> . . . buzzards! They'll be seen circling overhead. Everybody around'll know something's dead . . . something bigger'n a coyote. (He looks up at the sky then groans with relief.) They ain't spotted him yet. Lucky for me.

He is some time in getting the animals turned on the trail and headed back toward last night's campsite. Upon reaching it he ties a rope around the neck of each burro, fastens it to the burro ahead. Then he ties the lead burro to a tree. He takes the spade out of one of the packs and moves quickly to the task before him. Reaching the bush, he hesitates again briefly, then plunges ahead. CAMERA DOLLIES ahead of Dobbs as he pushes his way through, disregarding the brambles which tear his face and hands. When he gets to the place, Curtin's body isn't there. Dobbs cannot believe his eyes. He rubs them, then looks again.

DOBBS:
This was the place right here. I know it was.

Nevertheless, he begins to look around, crawling through the underbrush, spreading open the foliage, peering left and right and becoming more excited every second.

DOBBS:
He couldn't have flown away!

His nervousness mounts to the point of hysteria.

DOBBS (calls):
Curtin. Where are you? Curtin.

His voice comes bouncing back at him from a canyon wall—"Curtin. Where are? Curtin." The echo causes him a moment of real terror.

DOBBS (to himself):
I gotta get hold of myself. Mustn't lose my head. One thing, certain, he ain't here.

Dobbs's mind delves gropingly into the problem. Finally he comes up with a solution.

DOBBS:
I got it. The tiger. It dragged him off, that's what, to its lair. Very soon not even a bone will be left to tell the tale. Done as if by order.

The CAMERA PANS with him, laughing delightedly, as he starts out of the bush on back toward the campsite.

118.   PACK ANIMALS
as Dobbs comes up. Miraculously no accident has occurred in his absence. They are all in line waiting for the kicks that will set them in motion. These Dobbs delivers.

DOBBS:
Curtin didn't cry when I shot him. Not a sound

out of him. He just dropped like a tree falls. (After a moment.) Funny the way his legs and arms were twisted around. I could have laughed right out. (He chuckles.) Just to think, one slug and finished. A whole life. (He chuckles again; after a moment.) Tiger got him all right. Took him up in his jaws and carried him off. Must have been a big tiger—a royal tiger. They can jump over a fence with a cow in their mouths. (Suddenly.) His gun—it wasn't there either. No tiger would've taken that gun away . . . Maybe he's crawling around in the bush. If he reaches a village . . . nearest village is twenty miles. Take him two days anyway. That's all the start I need—. Vamos! Vamos! Pronto!

DISSOLVE TO:

119.   EXT. DEEP IN THE BUSH   NIGHTFALL

An Indian charcoal burner is tending his fire. A SOUND that is different from the other noises of the wilderness causes him to pause in his work and listen. Locating the sound, he picks a burning brand from the fire, reaches for his machete, and with cautious movements goes to investigate. The Indian pushes aside a heavy bough, revealing, in the flickering transient light of his torch, the figure of Curtin, all in rags and with a bloody head. Curtin looks at the Indian but does not seem to see. He keeps on crawling forward. After several moments, the Indian recovers from his initial bewilderment and calls for help.

INDIAN:

Hidalgo, ven pronto aquí. Ven a ayudarme.

Then he goes to the aid of Curtin.

INDIAN:

¿Pero qué le pasó, señor? ¿Lo atacó un tigre, o qué?

He raises Curtin's body, gets an arm over his shoulder, supports him out of the thicket. A second Indian appears from the bush on the opposite side of the charcoal fire. He also is dumbfounded at the bloody spectacle the white man makes.

FIRST INDIAN:

> Mira a este pobre hombre, parece extranjero y que lo atacó un tigre. Ayudame a llevarlo a la ranchería, ándale.[33]

They carry Curtin to the fire, lower him to the ground, then hurriedly set about cutting saplings to make a litter. As they are lifting Curtin onto the litter,

DISSOLVE TO:

120.   EXT. TRAIL   MED. SHOT   PACK TRAIN   DAY

Dobbs is driving the animals at a desperate pace, kicking them along and beating them with the flat side of his machete. The inevitable finally happens. One of the poor beasts goes down and cannot rise despite the blows Dobbs rains upon it. Even after his pack is removed, he will not get up. The other burros are too heavily loaded to take on the extra weight of what was in the fallen burro's pack, so everything in excess of the sacks of gold, a few hides, and a little water must be discarded.

DOBBS:

> I can't be more than three days from the railroad track. One water skin ought to see me through.

He goes to work rearranging the packs.

DISSOLVE TO:

121.   EXT. ADOBE HUT   HOWARD

ensconced on a hammock. The old man has obviously been leading the life of Riley. An Indian girl of fifteen or sixteen waves a leafy branch at him, keeping off the flies. There is a bottle of tequila beside him on the box. Without ever opening his eyes, Howard feels for

175

it, finds it, and raises it to his lips, thereby rinsing down the last of a whole roast chicken. OVER SCENE the SOUND of hoofbeats. Presently Howard's host appears with the Indian who discovered Curtin in the bush. He points at Howard saying: El señor es un gran doctor.

HOWARD (still not opening his eyes):
¿Qué dice, amigo?

HOST:

Oiga, señor doctor. Este hombre es de un poblado lejano y tiene algo de interés que contarle.

The Indian squats down in the sand beside Howard's hammock while the host continues the act.

HOST:

Lázaro, aquí, es carbonero. Andaba trabajando cuando oyó algo en la maleza. Creyó que sería un tigre pero al fijarse vió que era un hombre que se arrastraba, cubierto de sangre y casi muerto.

HOWARD (sitting up with a bound):
¿Cómo es ese hombre?

INDIAN:

Tiene el pelo castaño y ojos azules. Es muy alto y parece extranjero.

HOST:

Creo que es uno de sus compañeros.

INDIAN:

Está muy malo. Perdió mucha sangre. Si usted me acompaña pronto puede que le salve la vida.

HOWARD:
¿Me prestan un caballo?

HOST:
Seguro, y hasta vamos con usted.

CAMERA PANS with Howard and his host on their way to the corral. The host calls:

HOST:

Vamos todos a Zaputa, dónde está herido el amigo del gran doctor.[34]

They're on the horses in no time at all, and riding off agallop.

DISSOLVE TO:

122.   EXT. WILD AND ROCKY WASTELAND

Dobbs gets down on his hands and knees studying the map. His face is haggard; the cheekbones are more prominent than before and there is a frightened, haunted look in his eyes.

DOBBS:

I don't get it. (He looks around him.) Where's the Rio de la Saucella? According to this map I'm sitting on its banks with my feet in the water.

He takes the canteen off one of the burros, weighs it in his hands, and drinks sparingly. After he has screwed the cap on again and hung the canteen back in place, he looks around. A litter of brush and deadwood are piled up on either side of a narrow winding gully. Dobbs frowns. His mind is dull and he is slow to comprehend the meaning of what he sees. When he does he grunts, then whines slightly like someone who's been hit a hard blow in the stomach.

DOBBS:

This is the Saucella! . . . All dried up. The river that don't have any water in it in the winter.

He picks up the map with trembling hands, stares at it.

DOBBS:

Forty miles to Porla.

He turns back to the canteen, weighs it again in his hands, giving it a circling motion. The next instant he is kicking the burros savagely and shouting at the top of his lungs.

DOBBS:

> Get on, damn you. Vamos![35]

DISSOLVE TO:

123.   HOWARD

examining Curtin, washing his wounds, pouring tequila in him. Curtin's condition is greatly improved.

CURTIN (smoking a cigarette as he talks):

> I came to in the middle of the night. My gun was beside me on the ground. He must've left it there to make it look like suicide. There were four empty shells in it—only one live bullet. I figured he'd come back again in the morning to see if I still had a flicker of life. I thought of waiting for him and letting him have it, but there was a good chance, in my condition, I might miss, so I decided to crawl away like a poisoned dog.

HOWARD:

> Take it easy, son. You're talking too much.

CURTIN:

> Don't you worry about me. I'll pull out of this if only to get that guy.

HOWARD:

> So it appears our fine Mr. Dobbs has made off with the whole train and is on his way north.

Curtin growls.

HOWARD (continuing):

> Well, I reckon we can't blame him too much.

CURTIN:

> What do you mean by that?

HOWARD:

> I mean he's not a real killer as killers go. I think

he's as honest as the next fellow—or almost. The mistake was in leaving you two alone in the depths of the wilderness with more'n a hundred thousand between you. That's a mighty big temptation, believe me, partner.

CURTIN:

He shot me down in cold blood and after I was down, shot me a second time to make absolutely sure.

HOWARD:

If I were still young and I had been alone with you or him out there, I'd have been tempted too. Maybe I wouldn't have fallen, but I reckon I'd've been sure enough tempted. (He's put on the last bandage.) There. You're almost as good as new. Now to go and find that thief and get our goods back. (He turns to the Indians.) Si no llego a Durango para mañana noche perderé toda mi fortuna. Présteme un caballo. Se lo devolveré.

INDIAN:

¿Un caballo? Seguro que sí. Y vamos a ir con usted para que no le pase algo como a su compañero.

HOWARD (to Curtin):

Not only are they giving me a horse but they are coming along to keep me from any harm.

Curtin, sitting up, reaches for his clothes.

HOWARD:

You ain't coming.

CURTIN:

Who says so?

HOWARD:

We'll have some hard riding to do and you wouldn't be up to it. You're too weak.

CURTIN:
>   You aren't leaving me behind, see. (He gets to his feet, stands swaying in his weakness.)

HOWARD:
>   Look at you . . . weak as a newborn kitten. Don't worry. I'll do all in my power . . .

CURTIN (interrupting):
>   I'm going.

HOWARD (looks him up and down, then):
>   I reckon you're going.

He starts out of the room; Curtin follows.

>   DISSOLVE TO:

124.   LONG SHOT   PACK TRAIN
The trail has turned into a dirt road covered with fine dust. A plume of dust set up by Dobbs and the animals hangs in the air.

125.   CLOSE SHOT
Dobbs at the head of the train. The dust rises each time he puts a foot down. He is the same color all over—face, clothes, hands—the pale gray of the road. Only his eyes are different, appearing darker by contrast. Every so often a burro brays.

Dobbs is moving in a nightmare. At times the landscape revolves as though he were the center of a great turning wheel. Every so often the ground he is walking on rushes up at him and deals him a vicious blow in the face. Whenever this happens he must spit and blow to get rid of the dust that gets into his mouth and nose. Now and then he mumbles incoherently— his dry and thickened tongue and swollen lips are incapable of forming the sounds that make words. He is almost to the place before he knows: a clump of trees by a pool of brackish water. At first he thinks it is a trick of his mind—something conjured up out of his suffering. He rubs his forehead with the back of his hand, then, moving slowly, he leaves the road and passes into the cooling shade. The burros are before him to the water, their legs spread wide and their muzzles submerged. Dobbs gets down on his knees and drinks beside them. He splashes the water over himself. It's as though it had miraculous powers. He laughs with delight. It is only a little time before the madness goes out of his eyes. Dobbs addresses his reflection in the water.

DOBBS:
　Made it. I made it.

The reflection of another face shows in the pool above Dobbs's. The ugly, grinning face of a man wearing a palm leaf hat painted gold. Dobbs turns slowly around and gets to his feet. Behind Gold Hat two others are standing and they too are grinning.

GOLD HAT:
　¿Tiene un cigarro, hombre? Have you got a ciga-
　rette?

DOBBS (attempting nonchalance):
　No, I haven't, but I've got a few pinches of to-
　bacco if that will do.

GOLD HAT:
　And paper to roll it in?

DOBBS:
　I've got a bit of newspaper. (He takes a piece out
　of his pocket and hands it together with his to-
　bacco pouch to Gold Hat.)

GOLD HAT:
　Matches. (It's an order.)

Dobbs hands him a box of matches. Gold Hat lights up, then:

GOLD HAT:

> Going to Durango?

DOBBS:

> Yes. That's where I'm headed. I'm going to sell
> my burros. I need money. I haven't got a red
> cent.

Dobbs thinks he is being very clever in answering
thus.

GOLD HAT:

> Money? We need money too.

Gold Hat gives him back his tobacco pouch. Dobbs
leans against a tree and fills his pipe. He takes plenty
of time. He is trying to appear in no way worried or
afraid.

DOBBS:

> I could use a good mule driver—or two or three.

GOLD HAT (laughs):

> Could you?

Whenever Gold Hat laughs the other two do also,
even though they don't understand English.

GOLD HAT:

> How much is the pay?

DOBBS:

> Two pesos apiece. Of course I can't pay in ad-
> vance. I'll pay you when we get to town and I get
> some cash.

GOLD HAT:

> Sure . . . Are you alone?[36]

Dobbs hesitates, then:

DOBBS:

> Oh no, I'm not alone. Two of my friends are com-
> ing on horseback. They'll be here any minute
> now.

GOLD HAT:

That's funny . . . a man all by himself in bandit
country with a string of burros, his friends behind
him on horseback. (He addresses his two companions in Spanish.) Pablo, asómate al camino y vé si
vienen dos jinetes.

The second bandit gets up slowly, goes over to the
road, and looks toward the mountains.

SECOND BANDIT:

Han de estar más lejos de lo que el cree. Ni
siquiera el polvo se divisa.[37]

GOLD HAT (to Dobbs):

Your friends must be very far behind you. Pablo
cannot see any dust even from their horses. What
have you got in the packs? (He walks over to the
burros and with his fists pushes and pokes the
packs.) Seems to me like hides.

DOBBS:

It is hides. You're right.

GOLD HAT:

Ought to bring quite a lot of money.

Dobbs goes to one of the burros, tightens the straps,
then he turns to another and pushes against its pack
to see if it's still holding fast. Finally he tightens his
own belt, pulling his pants higher up, this to indicate
he is ready to make off.

DOBBS:

I guess I'll have to beat it now. How about it? Do
you want to come along with me and help with
the burros?

Instead of answering, Gold Hat winks at his companions. Dobbs sees the wink. His breath stops for a second, then he kicks the lead burro, starting the train

toward the road. The three bandits edge in among the remaining burros and take them by their halters.

DOBBS (shouts):

Get away from my burros.

GOLD HAT:

We can sell these burros for just as good a price as you'd get.

DOBBS:

Get away from those burros I tell you. (He draws his gun.)

GOLD HAT:

You can't frighten even a sick louse with that. (He points at the gun.) You can only shoot one and he won't mind much because the Federales are after him anyway, so what with your gun—we take that chance.

DOBBS:

Get back there from my burros.

Without waiting for the bandits to obey he aims at Gold Hat and pulls the trigger. But the gun clicks cold . . . twice . . . three times . . . five times. Dobbs stares at the gun in amazement. So do the three bandits. While Dobbs is remembering about the gun, one of them bends slowly down, picks up a heavy stone. Dobbs looks around frantically for another means of defense or escape. His glance falls upon the machete that is tied to the side of one of the burros. He leaps for it and grasps its haft, but as he goes to pull it out of its scabbard the stone crashes against his forehead. Dobbs falls. Before he can rise Gold Hat has the machete. Gold Hat springs at the fallen Dobbs, the machete upraised. THE REST WE SEE REFLECTED in the brackish waters of the pool: The stroke of the machete, then the figures of the three bandits standing, eyes downward, looking at something on the ground.

The water in the pool begins to darken. Gold Hat looks up from the ground to the machete in his hand. He touches his thumb and forefinger to the tip of his tongue, then he tests the cutting edge of the blade. The waters of the pool are growing darker and darker.[38]

In the excitement over stripping the body, the bandits forget about the burros who, paying no heed to what has happened, march off toward town. Gold Hat struts and swaggers around the pool admiring himself in Dobbs's pants, held up by Dobbs's belt. The other two are having an argument. Each has a shoe in his hand.

SECOND BANDIT:

Dame ese zapato, sinvergüenza. Es mío. Yo lo ví primero.

THIRD BANDIT:

A mí no me importa quien lo vió primero. Yo fui el que le dió el pedrazo que lo tumbó. A tí no te toca nada.

GOLD HAT:

Silencio, ladrones habladores. Vale más que se callen porque usaré el machete por segunda... y por tercera vez también. (Looking around he sees that the burros have gone off; he begins to roar.) Dónde están los burros... Ya se fueron al demonio. Andenle a traerlos, bandidos inútiles. Si llega uno al pueblo nos meterá en un cochino lío.[39]

126.   THE BURROS

moving briskly in the direction of the village, where they know from past experience food awaits them and much needed rest. The shadows are lengthening now and the evening wind is blowing in. When the three bandits finally catch up to the burros, the sun has disappeared behind the rim of the mountains to the west and night is beginning to fall. They drive the pack train off the road into a thicket of mesquite and get busy. The burros are unloaded and the packs are opened up. What they discover is a great disappointment to them.

GOLD HAT:

Estas pieles no sirven. Están llenas de agujeros. Están dadas a la desgracia. Si nos dan veinte pesos por todas será mucho.

The Second Bandit has found a number of bags made of rags and old sackcloth. Looking at them, he scratches his head.

SECOND BANDIT:

¿Qué demonios serán estos? Mira... (He pours the contents of one out onto the ground.) Uuuh... es arena... pura arena cochina... ¿Para qué diablos andaba cargando toda esta arena?[40] (He opens one bag after another, spilling the stuff out.)

Gold Hat, taking up a handful of it, looks at it closely and then tosses the stuff into the air. He shakes his head, makes a circling gesture with his forefinger at his temple.

127.   CLOSE-UP   THE YELLOW SAND
spilled on the ground, the wind blowing it.

DISSOLVE TO:

128.   EXT. TRAIL   NIGHT
HOWARD, CURTIN, AND INDIANS, ALL ON HORSEBACK
Two Indians riding ahead of the others rein in. When Howard and Curtin come up to them they discover, lying on the trail, a dead burro and the equipment Dobbs discarded. They exchange a significant look, then:

HOWARD:

How are you holding up?

CURTIN:
My shoulder's singing some but I'm okay.

They ride on.

DISSOLVE TO:

129.   EXT. PLAZA   VILLAGE   EARLY MORNING
The three bandits appear with their pack train. Gold
Hat hails an Indian youth crossing the plaza and goes
up to him. It is the same boy who, long months before, when the partners were just starting out, came
into the general store to tell them there were some
burros outside for them to look at.

GOLD HAT:
Oye muchacho. ¿Sabes quién quiera comprar
unos burros?

He walks around the burros inspecting the brands,
then casually he looks at the high boots which the
Second Bandit is wearing.

130.   CLOSE-UP
The high boots.

131.   INDIAN
looking at them. Now his gaze shifts to Gold Hat.

132.   CLOSE-UP
The belt with the silver buckle.

133.   INDIAN

YOUTH (when he is through with his inspection):
Pués puede que mi tío se los compre, si los vende
baratos. (He waves for them to follow him.) Vengan a la tienda de mi tío.

CAMERA PANS as they proceed across the plaza to the
general store. The youth hails the Storekeeper who
comes out.

YOUTH:

Oiga tío, estos hombres quieren vender estos burros.

The Storekeeper approaches the three strangers with dignity.

GOLD HAT (with a flourish):

Son magníficos burros, señor. Le garantizo que no los encontrará mejores en ninguna parte.

The Storekeeper examines them with the utmost care, and while doing so he discreetly notes the attire of the three mestizos. CAMERA CUTS from the boots to the uncle's sharp eyes, then to the trousers on Gold Hat. CAMERA MOVES UP to a close-up of the belt buckle.

STOREKEEPER:

¿Y cuánto pide por estos burros?

GOLD HAT (in Spanish; smiles craftily, narrows his eyes, trying to give the impression that he is a sly old horse trader well acquainted with all the tricks):

Doce pesos cada uno… Una ganga, entre caballeros.

STOREKEEPER:

Pués yo no puedo comprarlos todos, pero ya verá. Angel, llama a la gente del pueblo, pronto. Usted podrá venderlos al mejor precio. Así les irá bien a todos. (Angel gets up and leaves the group.) Mientras tanto pueden descansar. (He calls into the house.) Zeferina, trainos agua y unos cigarrillos.

Gold Hat and his companions squat down on their heels. A young girl brings out a pitcher of water, tobacco, and papers.

While they are rolling their cigarettes, the villagers begin to arrive. Oddly enough they all wear firearms or are carrying machetes. Observing this, the three companions glance nervously at each other. Not until the circle is complete and the three companions surrounded does the Storekeeper speak.

STOREKEEPER:
Amigos, aquí están tres individuos que vienen del valle a vender sus burros.

The three so introduced rise and greet the villagers.

BANDITS:
Buenas tardes, señores.

STOREKEEPER (suddenly to Gold Hat):
¿Y tienen fierro estos burros?

GOLD HAT:
Naturalmente que todos tienen fierro.

He looks around the burros to read the brand, but the villagers are standing in a way that covers them up.

STOREKEEPER (quietly):
A ver... ¿Cómo es?

GOLD HAT (uncomfortably):
¿El fierro?... Pués es... Bueno, usted sabe... es una rueda... con una raya, así. (He makes a sign with his fingers.)

STOREKEEPER (to one of the villagers):
A ver si es cierto.

VILLAGER:
No compadre, nunca.

The villagers laugh as though Gold Hat had got off a very good joke.

GOLD HAT:
Válgame, que memoria... Será el calor... quise decir... es una cruz con un círculo. (He also makes this sign in the air with his fingers.)

STOREKEEPER:
A ver si es cierto, amigos.

VILLAGER:
No compadre, menos.

This time there is louder laughter and more of it. Gold Hat looks around at his partners. His mouth is open and the sweat is pouring off him.

STOREKEEPER (taking a step forward):
> Usted no sabe el fierro porque no son suyos. Son de tres Americanos. ¿Y cómo se hizo de esas botas y los pantalones?

Gold Hat reaches back to his holster to pull his gun or rather the gun that had once been Dobbs's. To his surprise he finds the holster empty. The weapon is in the hands of the villager standing behind him. Again there is laughter and general merriment.

GOLD HAT (swings both fists and looks at the men around him as if he were threatening them all):
> ¿Esto es demasiado, pués de que se trata? Ni que fueramos bandidos.

STOREKEEPER:
> Pués precisamente, eso deben ser. ¿A poco no son los bandidos que asaltaron el tren, fueron capturados y después se escaparon?

The three do not wait for the next sentence. With one jump they break through the circle of villagers. They don't get very far. The villagers are after them instantly and the three companions are caught before they reach the line of adobe houses on the other side of the plaza. The villagers start tying them up.

STOREKEEPER:
> Esto compete a las autoridades militares. A ver, Angel, vé a avisar a la Guarnición, inmediatamente.[41]

DISSOLVE TO:

134. EXT. THE DUSTY ROAD OUTSIDE THE VILLAGE
CAMERA PANS with Howard and Curtin and their Indian escort. OVER SCENE the SOUND of a volley being fired. The troop of riders rein their horses in and listen.

CURTIN:
Shooting.

HOWARD:
Yeh—a volley. Execution probably.

INDIAN:
Sí, son los rifles de los Federales.[42]

They ride on, spurring their horses into a gallop. CAM-
ERA PANS them into the village. The plaza is deserted.
They ride to the other end of the plaza and take a dirt
road leading up to higher ground where a crowd has
collected.

135.   GRAVEYARD
Men and boys are shoveling dirt into three graves.
Those gathered look up at the approach of Curtin,
Howard, and the Indians. A voice hails them.

VOICE (OVER SCENE):
Ah... señores Americanos... ¡Cuánto gusto de
volver a verlos bien!

It is the Storekeeper, who comes forward with outstretched hands. Howard and Curtin dismount and
greet him.

STOREKEEPER:
Siento traerles muy malas notícias. Cerca de aquí
le pasó algo terrible a su compañero. Lo asaltaron
tres bandidos y lo asesinaron para robarle la ropa,
los burros y su carga.

CURTIN:
What's he saying?

HOWARD:
Dobbs is dead. Murdered by bandits.

STOREKEEPER:
Sin embargo, sus cosas están en un lugar seguro;
las pieles están en mi tienda y los burros en el
corral. Aunque esto es poco consuelo por la pérdida
de su compañero.

HOWARD (to Curtin):
> It seems all our goods are safe in his store but he realizes, of course, that that is poor consolation for the loss of our dear brother.

STOREKEEPER:
> Favor de pasar a mi tienda.

He leads the way and they follow. Curtin and Howard exchange a long look. The younger man raises his right hand. Howard sees that the fingers are crossed.

136.   THE GENERAL STORE
as he comes into view, followed by Curtin and Howard. On reaching the doorway the Storekeeper waves them inside.

137.   INT. STORE
In one corner there is a pile of saddles, hides, canvas coverings, an empty canteen, and several lengths of rope.

STOREKEEPER:
> Creo que no les faltará nada.

Howard and Curtin go to the corner and start burrowing in the pile. When they do not immediately find what they are looking for, they begin to fling things helter-skelter in the search.

CURTIN (finally):
> Not here . . . not here.

HOWARD:
> Keep your shirt on.

He turns to the Storekeeper.

HOWARD:
> ¿Sabe algo sobre unos costalitos, como así?... (he shows with his hands) ...y muy pesados?

The old man shakes his head slowly.

STOREKEEPER:
No, de eso no sé nada.

The youth who originally encountered the bandits in the plaza and led them to the Storekeeper steps forward from the group in the doorway.

ANGEL:
¿Dice usted, unos costalitos de lona?

HOWARD:
¿Sí, sí, dónde están?

ANGEL:
Pués no sé. No los ví. Yo sólo sé lo que dijeron los bandidos.

CURTIN (to Howard):
What's he saying?

Howard ignores the question.

ANGEL:
Dijeron que había unos costalitos con arenita que creyeron que eran para que pesaran más las pieles cuando las vendieran.[43]

CURTIN (wild):
What does he say? Tell me!

HOWARD (to Curtin):
The bandits thought they were bags of sand hidden in among the hides to make them weigh more when our dearly beloved brother went to sell them in Durango.

CURTIN (shouting):
But where are they . . . Where?

HOWARD:
Don't you understand? They poured our goods out on the ground. The wind has carried all of it

away—all of it to the four corners of Mexico.[44]
(He begins to laugh.)

STOREKEEPER:
¿Todo esta allí, verdad? ¿Sólo falta la arena?

HOWARD (laughing):
Sí... *s ó l o* falta la arena.

CURTIN:
What's that?

HOWARD:
He wanted to know if everything else wasn't there, and I told him yes, only the sand was gone.

Howard lets out such a roar of Homeric laughter that the Indians are startled by it, but after a moment, supposing that he is overjoyed by something, they fall in with him and laugh as heartily as he does.

HOWARD:
Laugh, Curtin, old boy, it's a great joke played on us by the Lord or fate or by nature—whichever you prefer, but whoever or whatever played it, certainly has a sense of humor. The gold has gone back to where we got it. Laugh, my boy, laugh. It's worth ten months of labor and suffering—this joke is.

Still laughing, Howard strolls out the door. After a moment Curtin moves after him.

CURTIN:
Well, what now?

HOWARD:
Far as I'm concerned I'm fixed for life—as a medicine man. I'll have three meals a day, five if I want 'em, and a roof over my head, and every now and then a drink to warm me up. I'll be

worshiped and fed and treated like a high priest
for telling people things they want to hear. A
good medicine man is born, not made. Come visit
me some time, my boy; even you will take off
your hat when you see how respected I am there.
Only the day before yesterday they wanted to
make me their Legislature—the whole Legislature.
I don't know what they mean by that but it must
be the greatest honor they can bestow. Yep, I'm
taken care of for the rest of my natural life. How
about you now? What do you aim to do?

Curtin rolls a cigarette, stands looking off into space.

CURTIN:

I dunno. Wish I did.

HOWARD (slaps him on the back):

Buck up. You're young—in years anyway. You
got plenty of time to make three or four fortunes
for yourself.

CURTIN:

The worst ain't so bad when it finally happens.
Not nearly as bad as you figure it will be before
it's happened. (He draws on his cigarette.) I'm no
worse off than I was in Tampico. All I'm out is a
couple hundred bucks, come right down to it.
Not very much compared to what Dobbsie lost.
(Nods.) Too bad about Mrs. Cody—I'm sorry
about our not being able to do like we planned.

HOWARD:

There's no place you're especially set on going to
is there?

CURTIN:

It's all the same to me where I go.

HOWARD:

Tell you what. You can keep my share of what
the burros and hides'll bring if you use the

money to buy a ticket to Dallas. Seeing her in person and telling her what happened would be a lot better than writing a letter . . . Besides, it's July and there might be a job for you in the fruit harvest . . . Well, what do you say?

The idea appeals to Curtin.

CURTIN:
I'll do it.

Howard takes the wallet and letter out of his pocket, gives them to Curtin. Then, Howard shakes hands with him briefly.

HOWARD:
Well, good luck.

CURTIN:
Same to you, old man.

They stand for a moment, hands joined, each trying to think of something further to say. Just about everything has been said. Howard lets go of Curtin's hand and turns to his horse and climbs into the saddle. His Indian companions also mount. Curtin watches them ride away. Once Howard turns and waves at him. Curtin waves back.

138. HOWARD AND THE INDIANS
walking their horses along the dusty road outside the village. Something blowing along the road catches his eye and he bends down from the saddle and picks it up. It is a canvas sack, torn and empty. Howard looks at it briefly, then throws it away. CAMERA FOLLOWS it as the wind picks it up and carries it off. OVER SCENE the SOUND of a harmonica.[45]

FADE OUT

THE END

Annotation to the Screenplay

1 In the film, the Depression-era reference to a "dime" has been dropped, and Dobbs makes a point of his nationality: "Hey, mister, will you stake a fellow American to a meal?"

2 In the film, this and all other references to Mexican expropriation of the oil fields has been cut.

3 The censors have toned down Dobbs's language in the film, changing "Mex" to "native" and "white man" to "an American."

4 Translation: BARBER: Will you have something on your hair, señor? To make it shine handsomely?
DOBBS: How much?
BARBER: Fifteen centavos . . . very good aroma.

5 Translation: Furnished Rooms for Rent.

6 In the film, Spanish music is heard in the background throughout this scene. A group of singers offscreen is performing a song, part of whose lyrics translate roughly as follows: "And when I am away from the one I love/ Madly in love with a woman,/ Only in drinking can I forget my anguish."

7 In the film, this speech has been cut.

8 In an earlier version of the script, as in Traven's novel, Dobbs leaves the Oso Negro to check on the results of the lottery. Here the appearance of the boy at a crucial moment makes the role of fate much larger.

9 Translation: VOICES: What happened? The train must have hit something. . . . No, not a wreck. Bandits. They're attacking the train.
HOWARD: On the floor, everybody. Lie down, quick.

10 The censors found this speech too explicit. In the film, Dobbs pauses meaningfully, his silence implying that he wants a woman. Howard then cautions him not to think about the subject too much.

11 Howard's speech is not in the film. See pages 20–21.

12 In Traven's novel and in the earliest versions of Huston's script, the soldiers are called Rurales, not Federales. Traven was apparently more sympathetic to the locals than to the national government.

13 This scene does not appear in the film.

14 In the film, Cody doesn't call down to the three prospectors. The

discussion of what to do about him goes further, Dobbs insisting on murder and Howard reluctant to accept that solution. Finally the question is left to Curtin to decide, and after some hesitation he sides with Dobbs—an important indication that he is not so free of greed and paranoia as he later claims. The three men then start up the hillside to shoot Cody, but are interrupted by the appearance of bandits.

15 In the film, a bit of dialogue from an earlier point in the script has been moved here to remind the audience of Gold Hat:

CURTIN: Howard, look, Howard. The one in the gold hat, remember?

HOWARD: Yeah, the man in the train robbery.

16 Translation: "Come here, boys, all of you. Hurry. A little birdie is sitting on its nest. What a great sight."

17 Translation: "All right. All right. Don't shoot, mister."

18 In the film, the prospectors are deadly accurate marksmen. Dobbs drills a hole in the bandit leader's hat, and Howard neatly hits the gold watch as it dangles from its chain.

19 In the film, the night attack has been omitted. When Cody is discovered with a bullet through the neck, Dobbs laughs: "Huh, one less gun."

20 This speech and the ones immediately preceding it do not appear in the film. See pages 20–21.

21 Howard's comments on providence have been cut from the film.

22 In the film, we do not see the photograph.

23 See page 19 for commentary on this letter. In the film, Howard reads badly and Curtin takes over for him.

24 This insert does not appear in the film.

25 In the film, Dobbs happily agrees to help repair the mountain: "She's been a lot better to me than any woman I ever knew. Keep your shirt on, old-timer. Sure, I'll help you." This sudden renewal of harmony among the miners is due in part to the realization that the work has been finished. In the novel, Traven comments that the three men, preoccupied with the problem of how to transport the gold safely, don't have time to bicker among themselves; it is the same with political states, he says, and as usual he draws a parallel between the miners and the society at large: "Any nation, regardless of political quarrels and fights for party supremacy, when confronted with war or the danger of losing her most important markets, unites under her leaders."

26 This scene, curiously reminiscent of a moment in William Faulkner's story "The Bear," does not appear in the film.

27 Translation: FIRST INDIAN: Good evening, men. Can we sit near the fire and rest a bit, please?
HOWARD: Sure, why not, friends. Would you like to drink some coffee with us?
FIRST INDIAN: Yes, thank you very much.

28 Translation: "I want some hot water. Some towels. Also a mirror and some tequila. You rub his hands and feet, immediately." In the film, Howard works alone in a large, clear space, surrounded by the entire village. See page 27.

29 Translation: INDIAN: Why are you leaving this locality so soon?
HOWARD: We have some important business to attend to in Durango.
INDIAN: Please, sirs. Don't leave so soon. We want you to stay with us for a few weeks.
HOWARD: Thanks for the invitation, but we must be in Durango in a week.

30 Translation: HOWARD: My highest reward was the pleasure of seeing the child open his eyes.
INDIAN: I have to pay my debt or all the saints in heaven will be angry. Please come.

31 This scene does not appear in the film.

32 Traven's handling of the equivalent scene is different in a few significant details. Dobbs accuses Curtin of having "Bolshevik ideas." Curtin is momentarily tempted by the chance to take Howard's gold: "He knew that the big oil magnates, the big financiers, the presidents of great corporations, and in particular the politicians stole and robbed whenever there was an opportunity." Like Dobbs, he becomes angry at having to do Howard's work, but is in more control of his emotions, noting privately that "something was wrong with Dobbs. He was not himself any longer."

33 In the film, this brief scene occurs *before* Dobbs learns that Curtin's body is missing. Translation: "Hidalgo, come here quick. Come and help me. . . . What happened, mister, were you attacked by a tiger, or what? . . . Here is a white man who looks like he's been attacked by a tiger. Help me carry him to the village, hurry up!"

34 Translation: HOWARD: What's going on?
HOST: See here, señor doctor, this man from a village over the mountains has something of interest to tell you. Lazaro, here, is a coal burner. He was deep in the bush when he heard something crawling along in the thicket. First he thought it might be a tiger,

but on looking closer he saw it was a man crawling on the ground, covered with blood and almost dead.

HOWARD: What does the man look like?

INDIAN: He has brown hair and blue eyes. He is very tall and looks like a foreigner.

HOST: I think it must be one of your companions.

INDIAN: He's very sick and has lost much blood. If you come with me quickly perhaps you can save his life.

HOWARD: Will you lend me a horse?

HOST: More than that, we'll go with you. Come, all you men. We're going to ride to Zaputa, where the great doctor's friend lies sick.

35 This scene does not appear in the film.

36 In the film, Gold Hat suddenly recognizes Dobbs: "Hey, did I know you from some place? Maybe I know you." A moment later he remembers: "I know who you are! You're the guy in the hole—who wouldn't give us his rifle."

37 Translation: GOLD HAT: Pablo, get out on the road and see if any horsemen are coming.

PABLO: They seem to be farther away than he thinks. I can't see any dust from their horses.

38 The staging of this scene in the film is somewhat different. See pages 29–30 for some of the details. We see Gold Hat giving Dobbs a couple of vicious blows with the machete, but our view of the murder is obscured by a burro in the foreground.

39 Translation: SECOND BANDIT: Give me that shoe, you dirty cheat. It's mine. I saw them first.

THIRD BANDIT: What difference is it to me who went for them first? I threw the stone that laid him out. You deserve nothing and you'll get nothing.

GOLD HAT: You're both low-down thieves and liars and you'd better stop your hollering or I'll use this machete a second time . . . and a third time, too . . . Where are the burros? Gone to hell. After them, you useless bandits. If even one of them reaches the village we'll be in a stinking mess.

40 Translation: GOLD HAT: The hides are no good—full of holes—all shot to pieces. We'll be lucky if we get twenty pesos for the whole lot.

SECOND BANDIT: I can't figure out what these are for. See. It's sand . . . just plain sand. Now what was he carrying all this sand for?

41 Translation: GOLD HAT: Listen, kid. Do you know anyone who might want to buy a few burros?

200

YOUTH: Maybe my uncle will if the price is reasonable. Come with me to my uncle's store. (To the Storekeeper.) Listen, uncle. These men would like to sell some burros.

GOLD HAT: Very fine burros, señor. I guarantee you, you cannot find better burros anywhere.

STOREKEEPER: How much are you asking for these burros?

GOLD HAT: Twelve pesos each, between brothers.

STOREKEEPER: I can't buy all the burros, but let's see what we can do. Angel, call together the people of the village. Hurry. You can sell your burros to the highest bidders. That'll be fair all around. Make yourselves comfortable in the meantime. Zeferina, bring out water and cigarettes. (To villagers.) Friends, here are three strangers who have come from the valley to sell their burros. Do the burros have a brand?

GOLD HAT: Naturally, they all have brands.

STOREKEEPER: What is the brand?

GOLD HAT: The brand . . . well . . . the brand is . . . Oh, you know . . . a circle and a bar.

STOREKEEPER: Is that right?

VILLAGER: No, compadre.

GOLD HAT: I was mistaken. It must be the heat. Now, strike me, how could I ever forget? Of course, the brand is a cross with a circle around it.

STOREKEEPER: Is that correct, amigos?

VILLAGER: No, compadre.

STOREKEEPER: You don't know how your animals are branded. The reason why is they are not your animals. They belong to three Americans. Now tell me where you got the boots you are wearing, and those pants?

GOLD HAT: You go too far. What is this anyway? Surrounding us as if we were bandits?

STOREKEEPER: It could not be, could it, that you are? You aren't, by any chance, the bandits who attacked the train and were captured and then escaped? This is a matter for the military authorities. Go, Angel, and tell them to come here at once.

42 In the film, we see the bandits dig their own graves and line up before a firing squad. Wind blows Gold Hat's sombrero away, and he stops the squad to retrieve it, putting it on before he lines back up to be shot.

43 Translation: HOWARD: Do you know anything about some sacks about this big? And very heavy?

STOREKEEPER: No, nothing.

ANGEL: What is it, are you asking about some sacks?

HOWARD: Yes, yes, where are they?

ANGEL: I couldn't tell you—I never saw them. All I know is what I heard from the bandits. . . . There were some bags filled with sand that your brother had put in among the hides so they would weigh more when he went to sell them.

44 In the film, Howard and Curtin ride to the ruins outside town, where they discover the torn bags. The wind, which has been blowing heavily in some of the earlier scenes, has now dispersed the gold.

45 The ending of Traven's novel is slightly different. Two bags of gold remain undestroyed. Howard and Curtin agree to remain where they are for a couple of months, and Howard offers to appoint Curtin as an assistant medicine man. In the completed film, the ending is both cynical and sentimental: Curtin waves good-by to Howard, who rides off with the Indians. Then, his arm in a sling, Curtin turns his horse and rides toward Texas. An insert shows a torn bag, once containing gold, blown to rest against a lonely cactus plant. Fade out.

Production Credits

Director	John Huston
Producer	Henry Blanke
Screenplay by	John Huston
Based on the novel by	B. Traven
Director of Photography	Ted McCord, A.S.C.
Art Director	John Hughes
Film Editor	Owen Marks
Assistant Director	Dick Mayberry
Sound Recorder	Robert B. Lee
Technical Advisors	Ernesto A. Romero and Antonio Arriaga
Set decorations by	Fred M. MacLean
Special effects by	William McGann, Director H. F. Koenekamp, A.S.C.
Make-up Artist	Perc Westmore
Music by	Max Steiner
Orchestrations by	Murray Cutter
Musical Director	Leo F. Forbstein

Handwritten annotations (right margin):
Across the Pacific, Red Badge of Courage, Key Largo, Moby Dick, African Queen, Judge Roy Bean, Life & Times of, The Man who would be King

East of Eden, Helen Morgan Story, The Sound of Music

Running time: 126 minutes
Released: January 1948

Cast

Dobbs	Humphrey Bogart
Howard	Walter Huston
Curtin	Tim Holt
Cody	Bruce Bennett
McCormick	Barton MacLane
Gold Hat	Alfonso Bedoya
*Presidente**	A. Soto Rangel
*El Jefe**	Manuel Donde
Pablo	Jose Torvay
Pancho	Margarito Luna
Flashy girl	Jacqueline Dalya
Mexican boy	Robert Blake
White Suit	John Huston
Flophouse bum	Jack Holt

*The discrepancy between the naming of these characters in the credits at the end of the film though not in the screenplay is here acknowledged but unaccounted for.

Inventory

The following materials from the Warner Library of the Wisconsin Center for Film and Theater Research were used by Naremore in preparing *The Treasure of the Sierra Madre* for the Wisconsin/Warner Bros. Screenplay Series:

Screenplay, no author indicated, no date, annotated, 152 pages.
Final, by John Huston, August 17, 1946, with changed pages to August 21, 1946, 141 pages.
Revised Final, by John Huston, January 10, 1947, with changed pages to June 9, 1947, 143 pages.

DESIGNED BY GARY GORE
COMPOSED BY CREATIVE COMPOSITION CO.
ALBUQUERQUE, NEW MEXICO
MANUFACTURED BY THE NORTH CENTRAL PUBLISHING CO.
ST. PAUL, MINNESOTA
TEXT AND DISPLAY LINES ARE SET IN PALATINO

⺋Ⱳ⺊

Library of Congress Cataloging in Publication Data
Huston, John, 1906–
The treasure of the Sierra Madre.
(Wisconsin/Warner Bros. screenplay series)
Screenplay by J. Huston, based on the novel
by B. Traven.
Includes bibliographical references.
1. Moving-picture plays.   I. Naremore, James.
II. Traven, B. Der Schatz der Sierra Madre. English
III. Title.   IV. Series.
PN1997.T67   812'.5'4   78-53298
ISBN 0-299-07680-6
ISBN 0-299-07684-9 pbk.

W W

The Wisconsin/Warner Bros. Screenplay Series, a product of the Warner Brothers Film Library, will enable film scholars, students, researchers, and aficionados to gain insights into individual American films in ways never before possible.

The Warner library was acquired in 1957 by the United Artists Corporation, which in turn donated it to the Wisconsin Center for Film and Theater Research in 1969. The massive library, housed in the State Historical Society of Wisconsin, contains eight hundred sound feature films, fifteen hundred short subjects, and nineteen thousand still negatives, as well as the legal files, press books, and screenplays of virtually every Warner film produced from 1930 until 1950. This rich treasure trove has made the University of Wisconsin one of the major centers for film research, attracting scholars from around the world. This series of published screenplays represents a creative use of the Warner library, both a boon to scholars and a tribute to United Artists.

Most published film scripts are literal transcriptions of finished films. The Wisconsin/Warner screenplays are primary source documents–the final shooting versions including revisions made during production. As such, they will explicate the art of screenwriting as film transcriptions cannot. They will help the user to understand the arts of directing and acting, as well as the other arts involved in the film-making process, in comparing these screenplays with the final films. (Films of the Warner library are available at modest rates from the United Artists nontheatrical rental library, United Artists/16 mm.)

From the eight hundred feature films in the library, the general editor and the editorial committee of the series have chosen those that have received critical recognition for their excellence of directing, screenwriting, and acting, films that are distinctive examples of their genre, those that have particular historical relevance, and some that are adaptations of well-known novels and plays. The researcher, instructor, or student can, in the judicious selection of individual volumes for close examination, gain a heightened appreciation and broad understanding of the American film and its historical role during this critical period.